THE ESSENTIAL GUIDE TO BLACKLETTER ALPHABETS FOR LETTERING ARTISTS, CALLIGRAPHERS AND DESIGNERS

VINTAGE DESIGNS

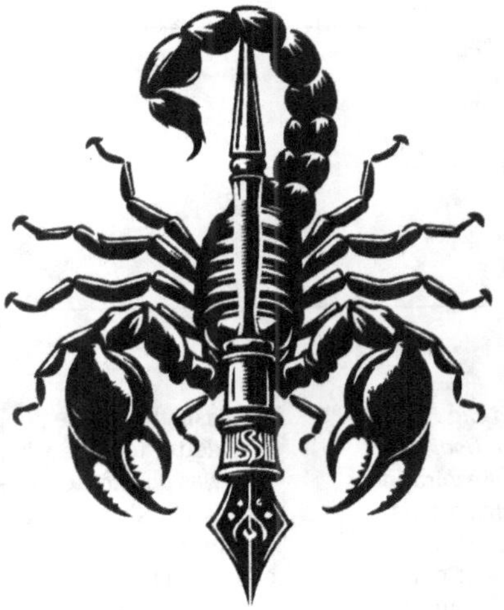

Blackletter

And Old English Lettering

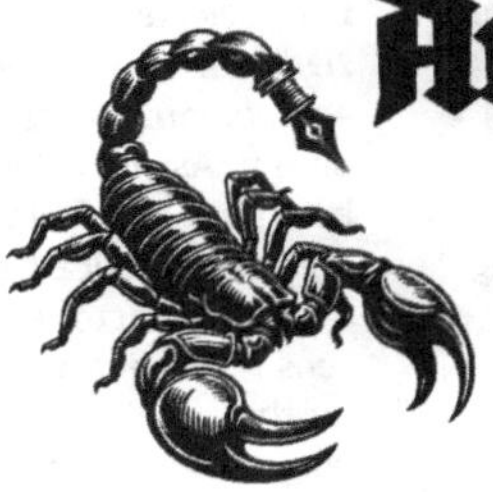

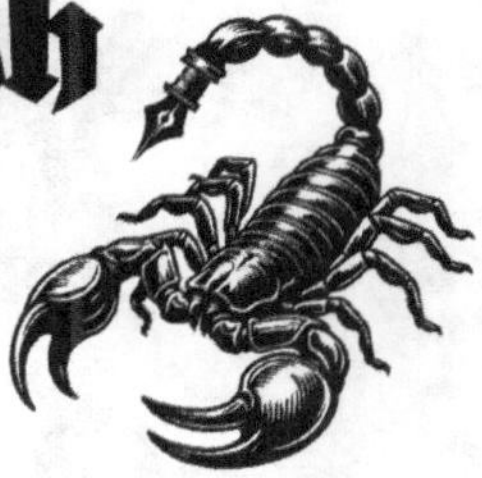

A REFERENCE BOOK   FOR TYPOGRAPHERS   BY VAULT EDITIONS

VOL | 126 ALPHABETS | DOWNLOAD INCLUDED | HIGH-RESOLUTION | ONE

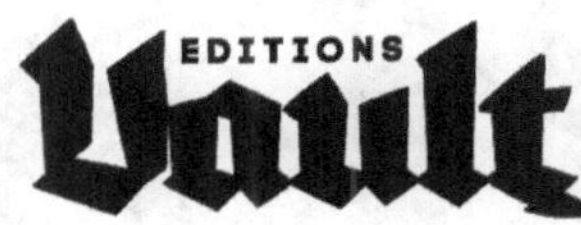

EDITIONS
Vault

BIBLIOGRAPHICAL NOTE

This publication is a new work by Vault Editions Ltd.

AUTHOR

This publication was curated and authored by Kale James.

I N T R O D U C T I O N

PREFACE

By Kale James

The Blackletter and Old English Lettering Reference Book is a comprehensive and inspirational reference for lettering artists, calligraphers, typographers, and designers. This book celebrates the rich heritage and enduring allure of Blackletter script, showcasing an impressive array of 126 alphabets, each with unique character and historical significance.

The story of Blackletter script begins in the mid-12th century, emerging in Western Europe as a response to an increasingly literate population. Blackletter text grew in popularity as it was quicker to transcribe than it's predecessor, and was used to create religious, educational, and literary texts during the medieval period. The name Blackletter is often considered a reference to the script's dark, dense appearance, contrasting to the white page.

The Old English script is a derivative of Blackletter that was popular in England for hundreds of years because it was easy to read and reproduce. It was used in a range of texts, from 13th-century religious and educational books to 18th-century joke books and romances, which were widely distributed and read by the common people.

This book will take you on a historical journey, exploring various styles and iterations of Blackletter alphabets and the four primary styles of Blackletter text: Textura, Rotunda, Bastarda and Fraktur. This book serves as a catalogue of styles and a source of inspiration, encouraging modern creatives to explore and reinterpret these historical scripts in contemporary design.

Our goal is to provide a resource that is both educational and inspiring. Whether you are a seasoned professional or a curious enthusiast, this book offers a window into the fascinating world of blackletter scripts. It is an invitation to appreciate the beauty of these alphabets and to carry forward their legacy in your creative pursuits.

In this meticulously curated collection, each alphabet has been selected for its historical significance, aesthetic appeal, and potential to inspire modern design. As you delve into this book, you will find that each alphabet's intricate details and unique characteristics evoke a sense of inspiration and respect for the craftsmanship of those who designed them. This journey is not just about revisiting history; it's about rediscovering these alphabets' timeless beauty and versatility in a contemporary context, and we hope each page is a testament to the enduring legacy of Blackletter scripts.

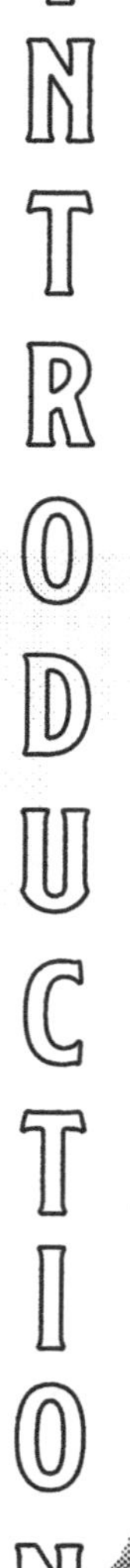

PUBLISHER	ISBN	
Vault Editions Ltd vaulteditions.com	978-1-922966-29-2	vau...

TABLE OF CONTENTS

Deiter Steffan	01-89
Peter Wiegel	90-118
Michael Stutz	119
Joseph Warren Phinney	120
Bumbayo Font Fabrik	121
Kevin King	122
J. Mach Wust	123-124
ANRT	125
Fredrich R. Brennan	126

ACKNOWLEDGMENTS

This book is a tribute to the enduring legacy of blackletter scripts. Its realisation would not have been possible without the contributions of numerous talented individuals and their passion for typography. In particular, we extend our deepest gratitude and acknowledgement to two remarkable typographers, Dieter Steffmann and Peter Wiegel, whose vast and exceptional body of work has significantly enriched this collection.

Dieter Steffmann's mastery of typography, especially in historical and blackletter typefaces, has been an invaluable resource. His dedication to the craft and his profound ability to breathe life into historic scripts have been instrumental in preserving and promoting this art form, and his work will continue to inspire generations of typographers and designers.

Peter Wiegel's extraordinary contributions are hugely influential. His meticulous attention to detail and commitment to reviving historical typefaces reflects a deep understanding of the nuances of blackletter scripts, making them accessible and relevant in the modern era. We are immensely grateful for his relentless pursuit of typographic excellence.

In addition to these luminaries, this book features the work of many other talented typographers, each of whom has brought their unique vision and expertise to the fore. Their collective efforts have created a rich tapestry of styles and interpretations, showcasing the versatility and beauty of blackletter alphabets. We extend our heartfelt thanks to all these artists for their remarkable contributions. Their dedication to their craft not only honours the past but also paves the way for innovative expressions in the future.

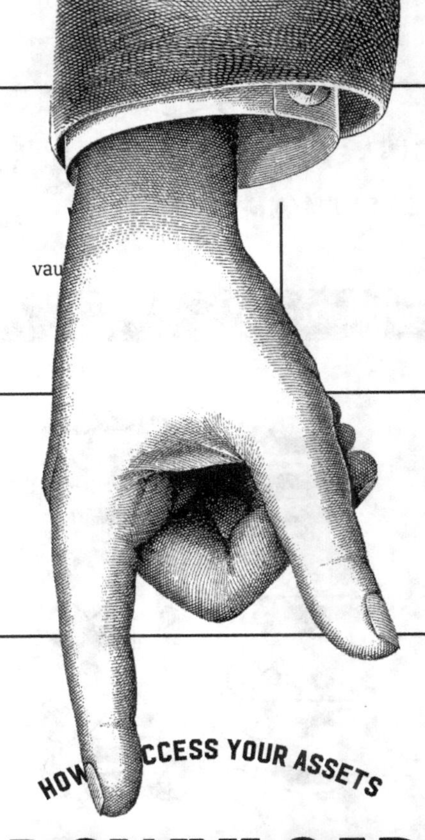

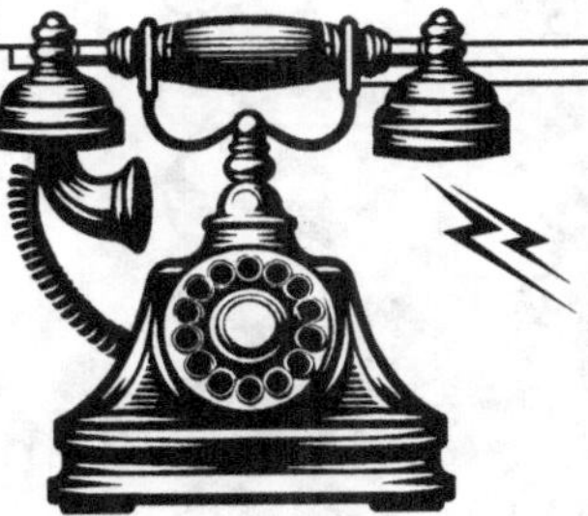

CONTACT

Do you need assistance accessing your files? Or do you have a questions about our products and services? If so, our team will be more than happy to help you. Please contact Vault Editions via: info@vaulteditions.com

01

A B C D E F G H I J K L M
N O P Q R S T U V W X Y Z
a b c d e f g h i j k l m n o p q r s t u
v w x y z
1 2 3 4 5 6 7 8 9 0

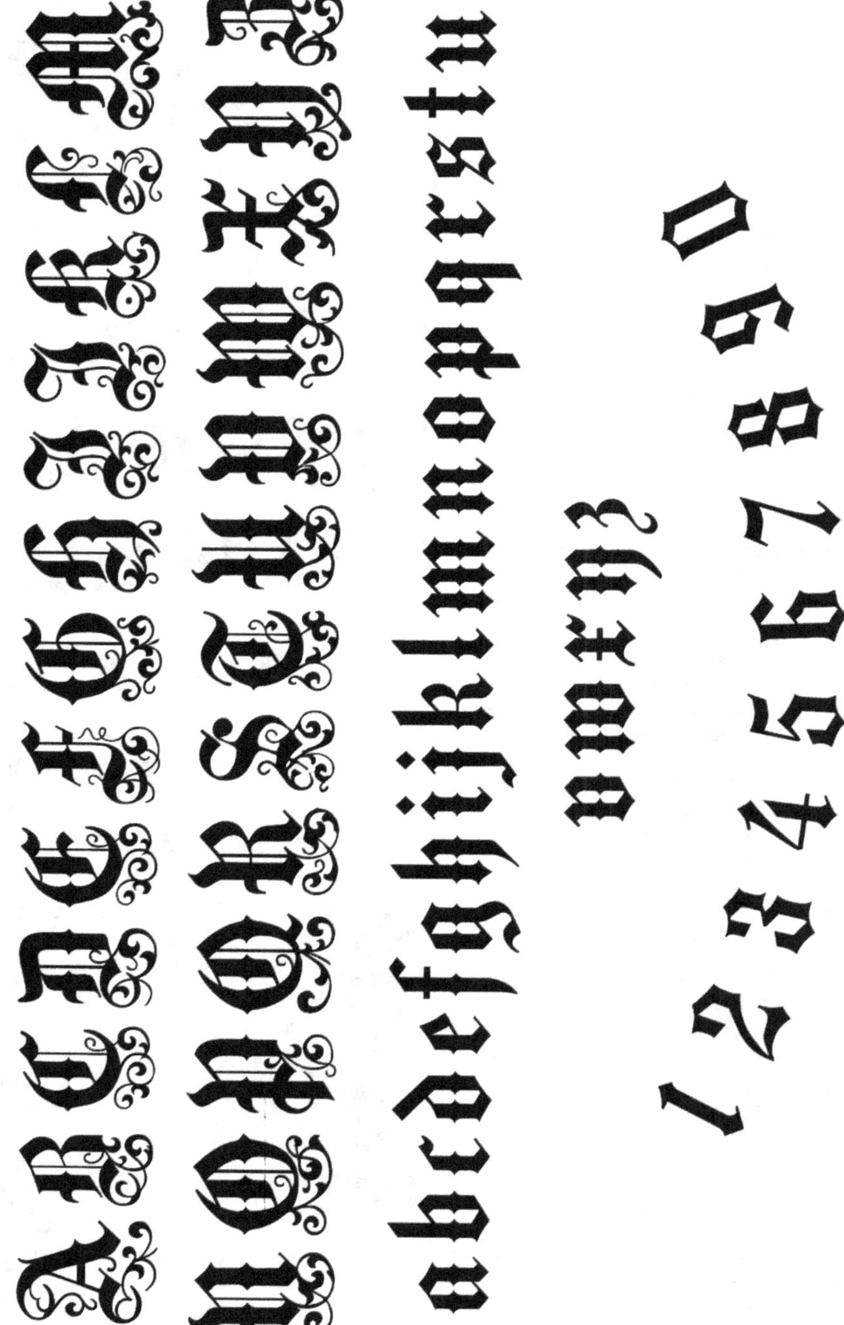

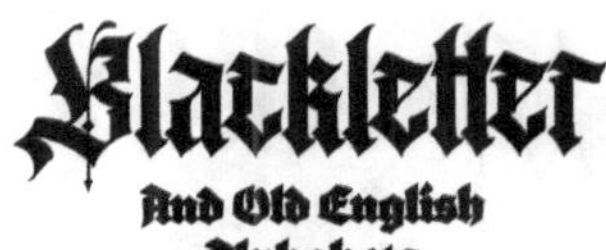

UPPER | LOWER | NUMERALS ⟷ WEIGHT: REGULAR ⟷ POINT SIZE: 82

02

abcdefghijklmnopqrstu
vwxyz

0123456789

A HIGH RESOLUTION FILE OF THIS
SPECIMEN SHEET CAN BE DOWNLOADED
FROM THE VAULT EDITIONS' WEBSITE.

Vault Editions Ltd

PRACTICE
MAKES
PERFECT
T R D   M R K

INDUSTRY STD

VAULTEDITIONS.COM

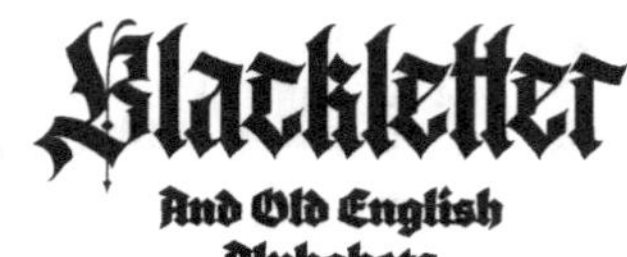

UPPER | LOWER | NUMERALS   WEIGHT: REGULAR   POINT SIZE: 81

03

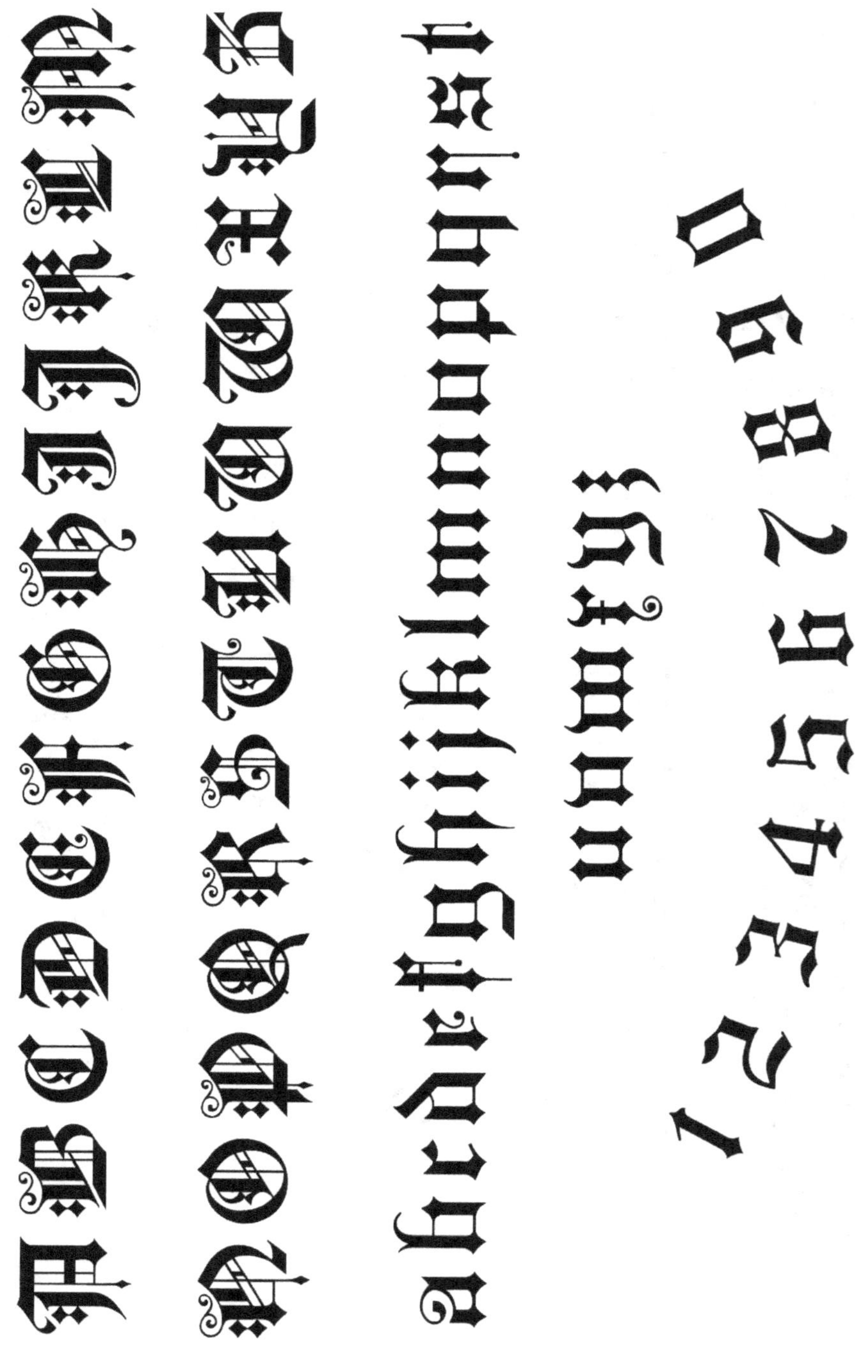

A HIGH RESOLUTION FILE OF THIS SPECIMEN SHEET CAN BE DOWNLOADED FROM THE VAULT EDITIONS' WEBSITE.

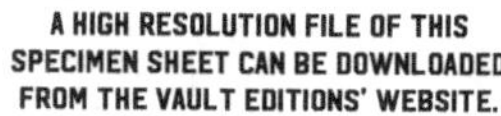

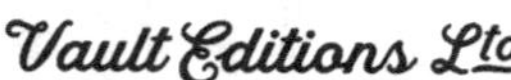

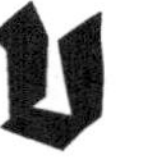

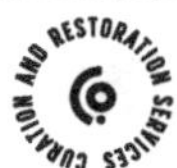

INDUSTRY STD

VAULTEDITIONS.COM

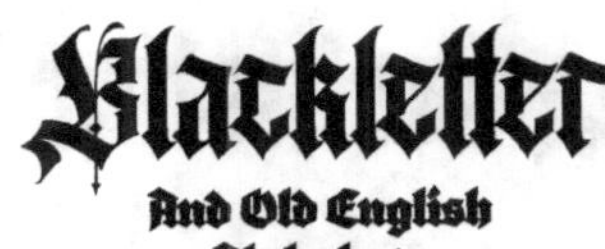

.TYPEFACE.
HARROWGATE

UPPER | LOWER | NUMERALS   ⟷   WEIGHT: REGULAR   ⟷   POINT SIZE: 80

04

A HIGH RESOLUTION FILE OF THIS SPECIMEN SHEET CAN BE DOWNLOADED FROM THE VAULT EDITIONS' WEBSITE.

Vault Editions Ltd

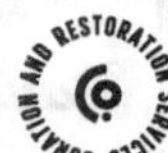

INDUSTRY STD

VAULTEDITIONS.COM

05

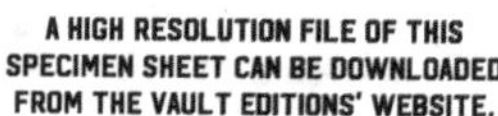

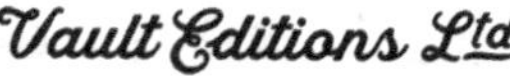

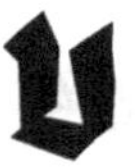

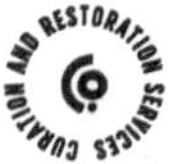

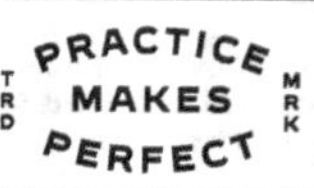

INDUSTRY STD

VAULTEDITIONS.COM

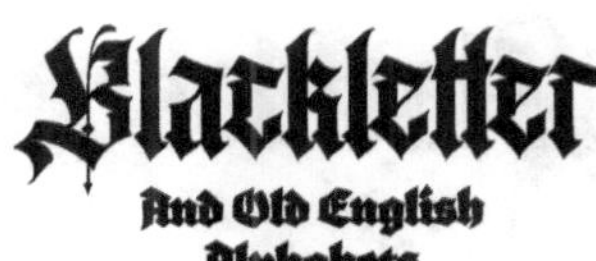

Blackletter
And Old English
Alphabets

06

ABCDEFGHIJKLM
NOPQRSTUVWXYZ

abcdefghijklmnopqrst
uvwxyz

1234567890

Vault Editions Ltd

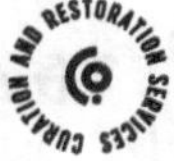

PRACTICE MAKES PERFECT

INDUSTRY STD

VAULTEDITIONS.COM

.DESIGNER.
DIETER STEFFMANN

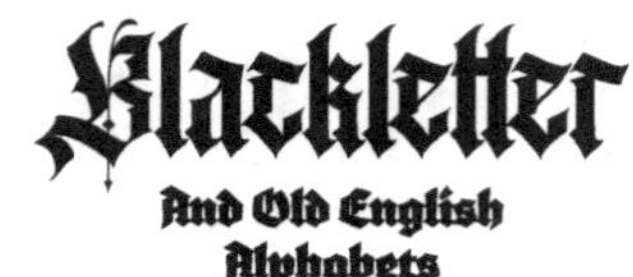

.TYPEFACE.
BLACKWOOD CASTLE

UPPER | LOWER | NUMERALS　　WEIGHT: REGULAR　　POINT SIZE: 82

ABCDEFGHIJKLM
NOPQRSTUVWXYZ
abcdefghijklmnopqrst
uvwxyz
1234567890

Vault Editions Ltd

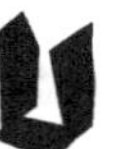
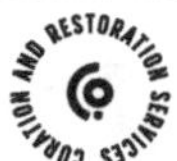

PRACTICE
MAKES
PERFECT

INDUSTRY STD

VAULTEDITIONS.COM

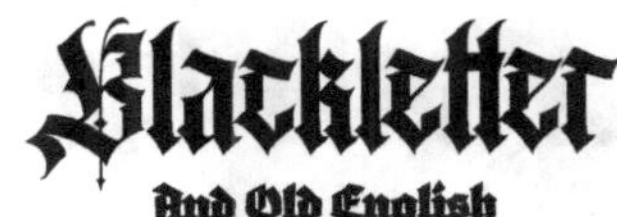

08

A B C D E F G H I J K L M
N O P Q R S T U V W X Y Z

a b c d e f g h i j k l m n o p q r s t u
v w x y z

1 2 3 4 5 6 7 8 9 0

Vault Editions Ltd 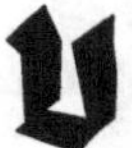 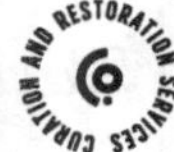

PRACTICE MAKES PERFECT

INDUSTRY STD

VAULTEDITIONS.COM

09

A B C D E F G H I J K L M N
O P Q R S T U V W X Y Z
a b c d e f g h i j k l m n o p q r s t u
v w x y z
1 2 3 4 5 6 7 8 9 0

Vault Editions Ltd

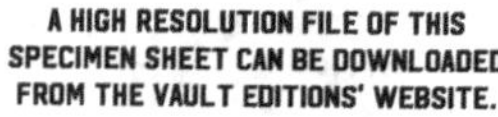
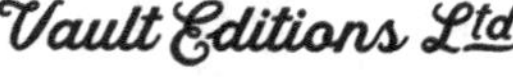
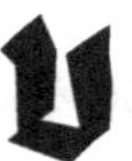
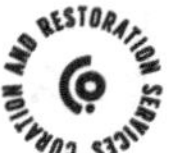

INDUSTRY STD

VAULTEDITIONS.COM

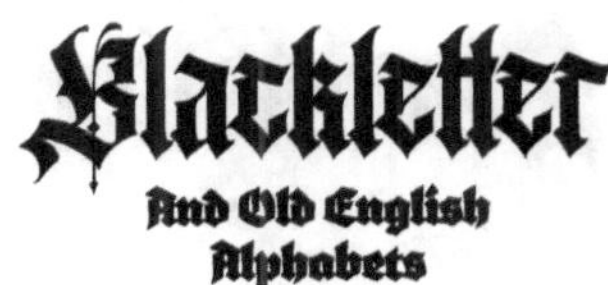

.TYPEFACE.

ENGLISH TOWNE

UPPER | LOWER | NUMERALS   WEIGHT: REGULAR   POINT SIZE: 79

ABCDEFGHIJKLM
NOPQRSTUVWXYZ
abcdefghijklmnopqrst
uvwxyz
1234567890

Vault Editions Ltd

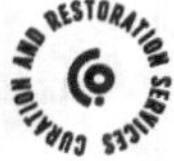

PRACTICE MAKES PERFECT
TRD   MRK

INDUSTRY STD

VAULTEDITIONS.COM

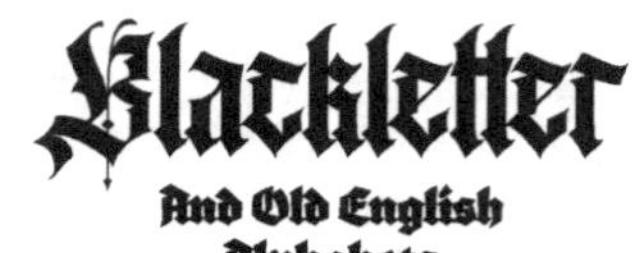

UPPER | LOWER | NUMERALS   ⟵——⟶   WEIGHT: REGULAR   ⟵——⟶   POINT SIZE: 84

11

ABCDEFGHIJKLM
NOPQRSTUVWXYZ
abcdefghijklmnopqrstu
vwxyz
1234567890

Vault Editions Ltd

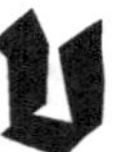

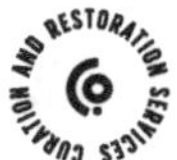

PRACTICE MAKES PERFECT

INDUSTRY STD

VAULTEDITIONS.COM

UPPER | LOWER | NUMERALS WEIGHT: REGULAR POINT SIZE: 80

A B C D E F G H I J K L M N O P Q R S T U V W X Y Z

a b c d e f g h i j k l m n o p q r s t u v w x y z

1 2 3 4 5 6 7 8 9 0

Vault Editions Ltd

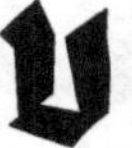
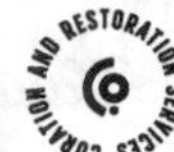

PRACTICE MAKES PERFECT

INDUSTRY STD

VAULTEDITIONS.COM

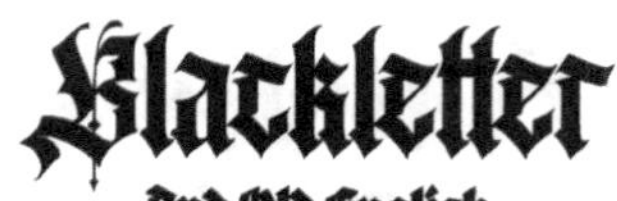

UPPER | LOWER | NUMERALS ⟷	WEIGHT: REGULAR ⟷	POINT SIZE: 80

13

𝕬𝕭𝕮𝕯𝕰𝕱𝕲𝕳𝕴𝕵𝕶𝕷𝕸

𝕹𝕺𝕻𝕼𝕽𝕾𝕿𝖀𝖁𝖂𝖃𝖄𝖅

abcdefghijklmnopqrst
uvwxyz

1 2 3 4 5 6 7 8 9 0

Vault Editions Ltd

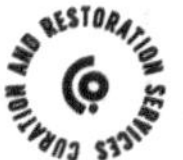

PRACTICE
MAKES
PERFECT
T R D · M R K

INDUSTRY STD

VAULTEDITIONS.COM

.DESIGNER.
DIETER STEFFMANN

Blackletter
And Old English
Alphabets

.TYPEFACE.
OLD ENGLISH FIVE

UPPER | LOWER | NUMERALS   WEIGHT: REGULAR   POINT SIZE: 79

ABCDEFGHIJKLM
NOPQRSTUVWXYZ
abcdefghijklmnopqrstu
vwxyz
1234567890

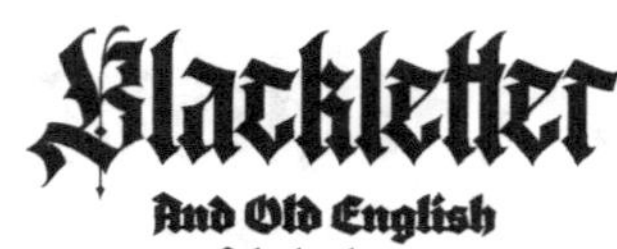

UPPER | LOWER | NUMERALS   ←→   WEIGHT: REGULAR   ←→   POINT SIZE: 81

15

ABCDEFGHIJKLMN
OPQRSTUVWXYZ
abcdefghijklmnopqr
stuvwxyz
1234567890

Vault Editions Ltd

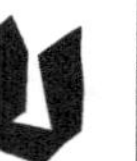
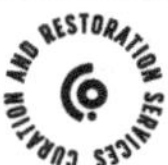

PRACTICE MAKES PERFECT
T R D   M R K

INDUSTRY STD
VAULTEDITIONS.COM

Blackletter
And Old English Alphabets

UPPER | LOWER | NUMERALS ⟷ WEIGHT: REGULAR ⟷ POINT SIZE: 81

16

A B C D E F G H I J K L M N
O P Q R S T U V W X Y Z
a b c d e f g h i j k l m n o p q r s t
u v w x y z
1 2 3 4 5 6 7 8 9 0

Vault Editions Ltd

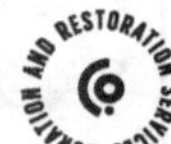

CURATION AND RESTORATION SERVICES

PRACTICE MAKES PERFECT
TRD · MRK

INDUSTRY STD

VAULTEDITIONS.COM

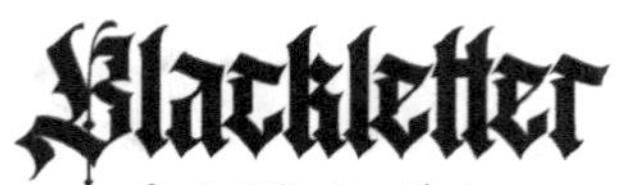

Blackletter
And Old English Alphabets

UPPER | LOWER | NUMERALS ⟷ WEIGHT: REGULAR ⟷ POINT SIZE: 81

17

A B C D E F G H I J K L M
N O P Q R S T U V W X Y Z
a b c d e f g h i j k l m n o p q r s t u v w x y z
1 2 3 4 5 6 7 8 9 0

Vault Editions Ltd 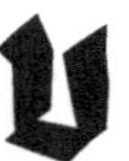

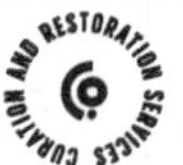

PRACTICE MAKES PERFECT

INDUSTRY STD

VAULTEDITIONS.COM

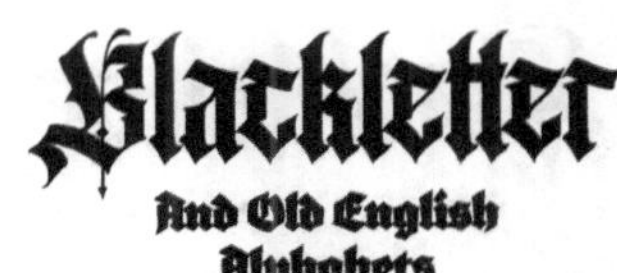

.DESIGNER.
DIETER STEFFMANN

.TYPEFACE.
HANSA GOTISCH

UPPER | LOWER | NUMERALS ⟵⟶ WEIGHT: REGULAR ⟵⟶ POINT SIZE: 83

A B C D E F G H I J K L M
N O P Q R S T U V W X Y Z

a b c d e f g h i j k l m n o p q r s t u v
w x y z

0 6 8 2 9 5 4 3 2 1

Vault Editions Ltd

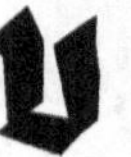
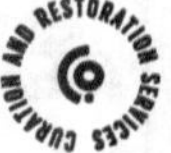

PRACTICE MAKES PERFECT
CURATION AND RESTORATION SERVICES

INDUSTRY STD

VAULTEDITIONS.COM

.DESIGNER.
DIETER STEFFMANN

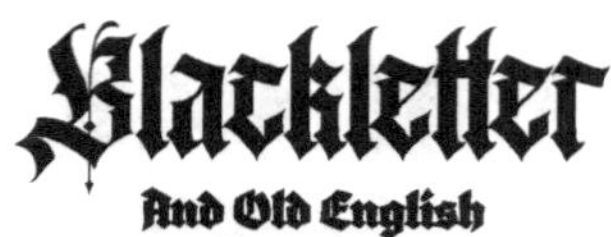

.TYPEFACE.
GRUSSHARTEN GOTISCH

UPPER | LOWER | NUMERALS   WEIGHT: REGULAR   POINT SIZE: 82

ABCDEFGHIJKLM
NOPQRSTUVWXYZ

abcdefghijklmnopqrstuvw
xyz

1234567890

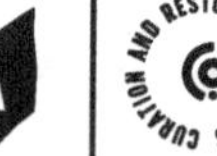

Vault Editions Ltd

CURATION AND RESTORATION SERVICES

PRACTICE MAKES PERFECT

INDUSTRY STD

VAULTEDITIONS.COM

UPPER | LOWER | NUMERALS ⟷ WEIGHT: REGULAR ⟷ POINT SIZE: 81

ABCDEFGHIJKLM
NOPQRSTUVWXYZ
abcdefghijklmnopqrstu
vwxyz
1234567890

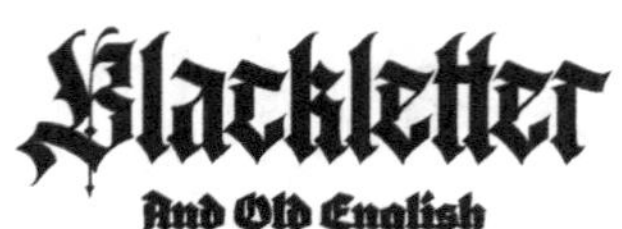

.DESIGNER.
DIETER STEFFMANN

.TYPEFACE.
GOTENBURG

UPPER | LOWER | NUMERALS ⟷ WEIGHT: REGULAR ⟷ POINT SIZE: 82

ABCDEFGHIJKLM
NOPQRSTUVWXYZ
abcdefghijklmnopqrstu
vwxyz
1234567890

A HIGH RESOLUTION FILE OF THIS
SPECIMEN SHEET CAN BE DOWNLOADED
FROM THE VAULT EDITIONS' WEBSITE.

Vault Editions Ltd

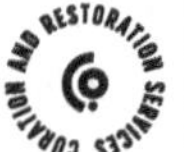

PRACTICE
MAKES
PERFECT

INDUSTRY STD

VAULTEDITIONS.COM

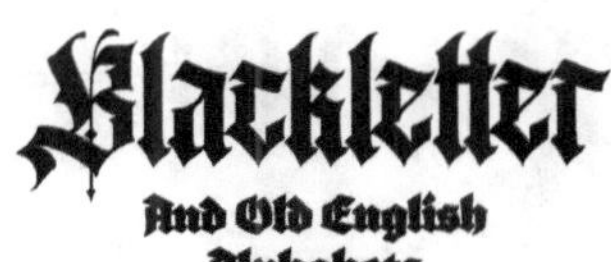

UPPER | LOWER | NUMERALS WEIGHT: REGULAR POINT SIZE: 82

ABCDEFGHIJKLMN
OPQRSTUVWXYZ
abcdefghijklmnopqr
stuvwxyz
1234567890

A HIGH RESOLUTION FILE OF THIS SPECIMEN SHEET CAN BE DOWNLOADED FROM THE VAULT EDITIONS' WEBSITE.

Vault Editions Ltd

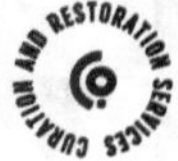

PRACTICE MAKES PERFECT
T R D   M R K

INDUSTRY STD

VAULTEDITIONS.COM

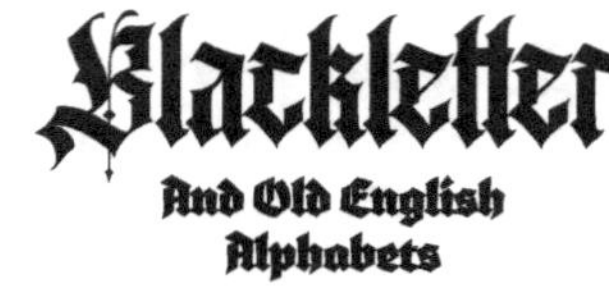

23

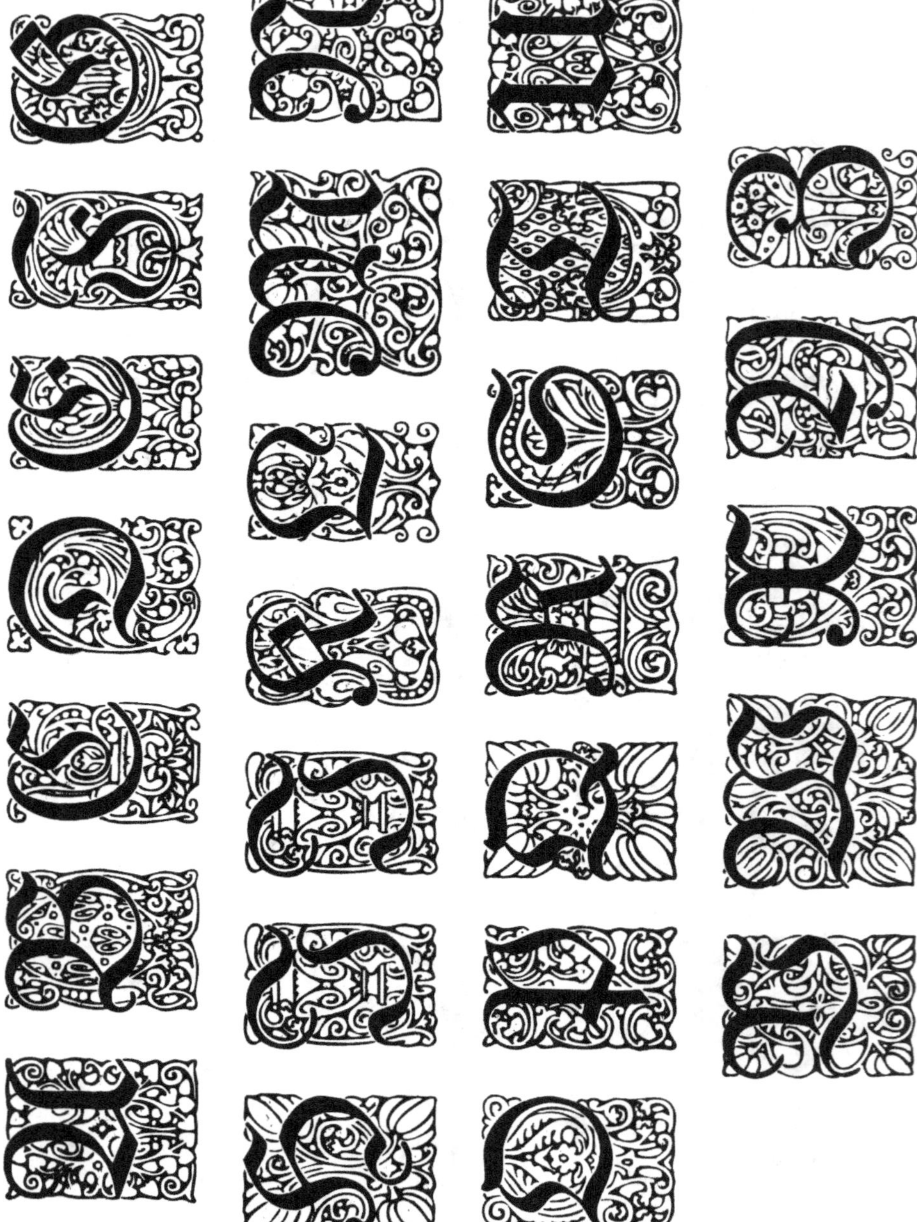

Vault Editions Ltd

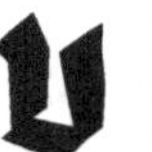
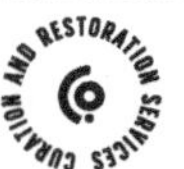

PRACTICE MAKES PERFECT

INDUSTRY STD

VAULTEDITIONS.COM

.DESIGNER.
DIETER STEFFMANN

Blackletter
And Old English
Alphabets

.TYPEFACE.
DUERER GOTISCH

UPPER | LOWER | NUMERALS ⟷ WEIGHT: REGULAR ⟷ POINT SIZE: 81

A HIGH RESOLUTION FILE OF THIS SPECIMEN SHEET CAN BE DOWNLOADED FROM THE VAULT EDITIONS' WEBSITE.

Vault Editions Ltd

CURATION AND RESTORATION SERVICES

PRACTICE MAKES PERFECT
T R D / M R K

INDUSTRY STD

VAULTEDITIONS.COM

25

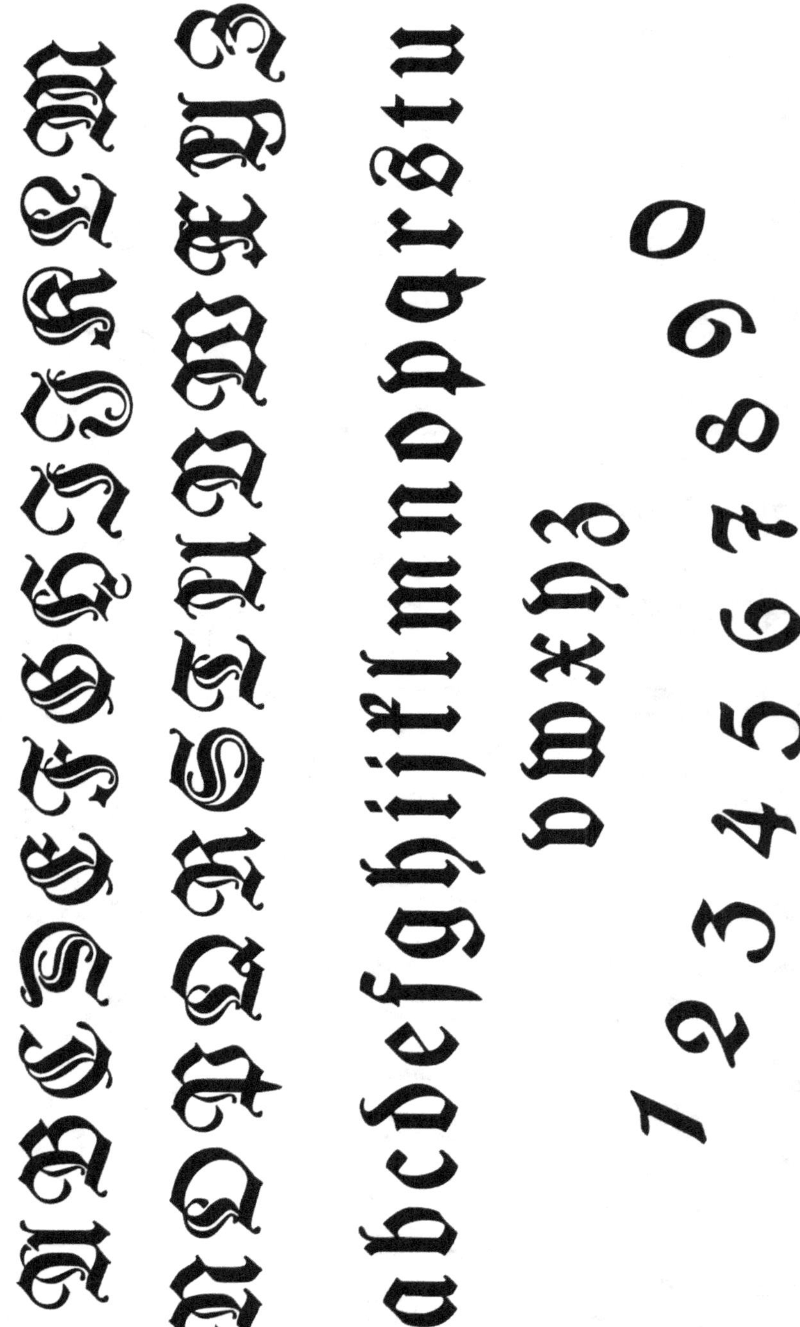

Vault Editions Ltd

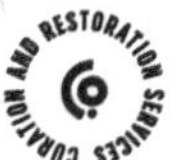

CURATION AND RESTORATION SERVICES

PRACTICE MAKES PERFECT

INDUSTRY STD

VAULTEDITIONS.COM

.DESIGNER.
DIETER STEFFMANN

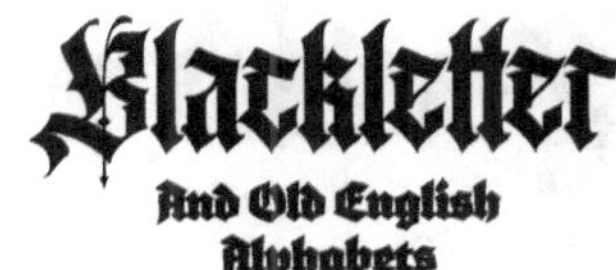
Blackletter
And Old English
Alphabets

.TYPEFACE.
**WIEYNK FRAKTUR
INITIALEN**

UPPER | LOWER | NUMERALS ←——→ WEIGHT: REGULAR ←——→ POINT SIZE: 82

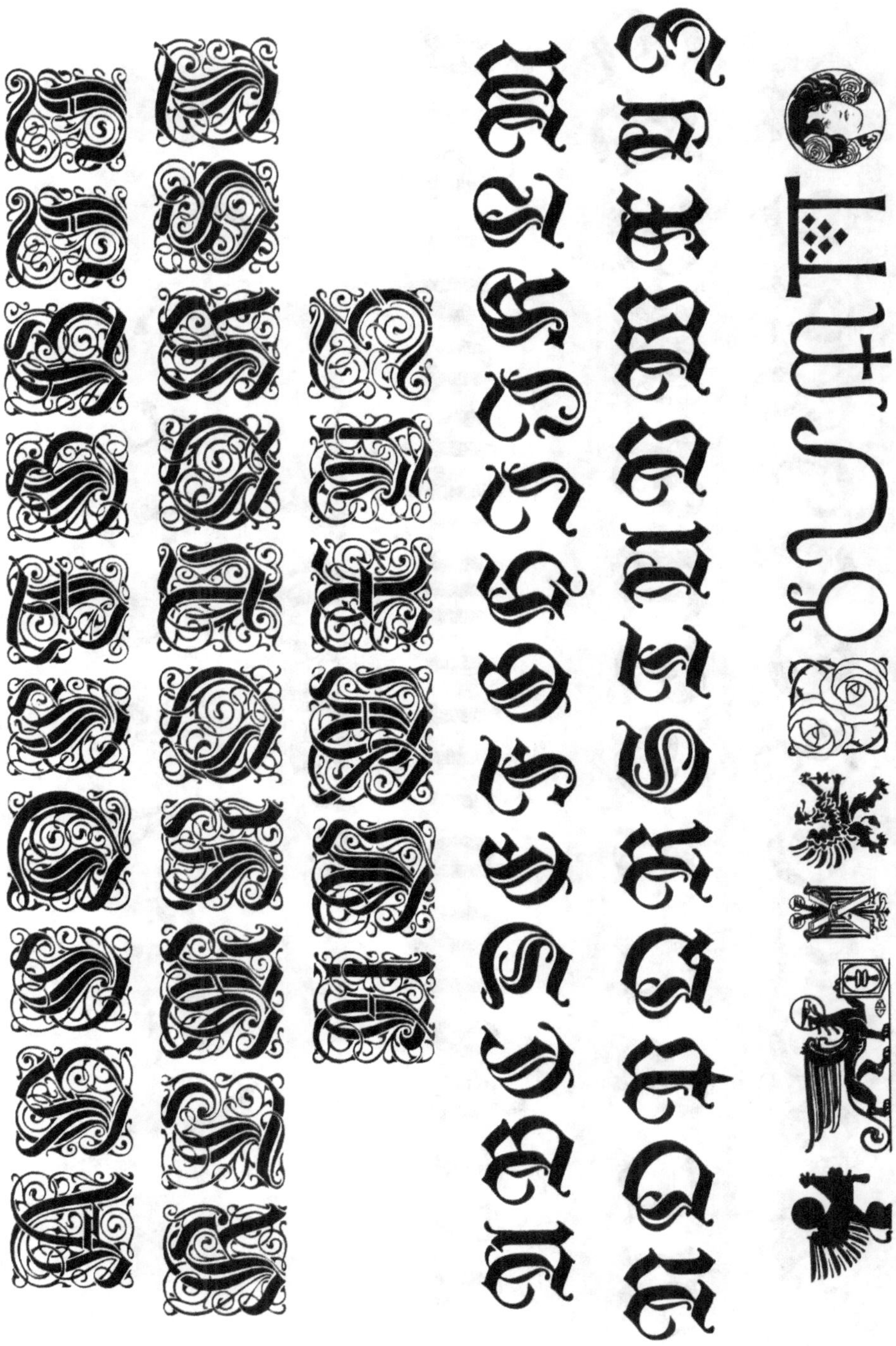

A HIGH RESOLUTION FILE OF THIS SPECIMEN SHEET CAN BE DOWNLOADED FROM THE VAULT EDITIONS' WEBSITE.

Vault Editions Ltd

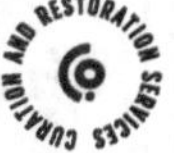

CURATION AND RESTORATION SERVICES

PRACTICE
MAKES
PERFECT
TRD MRK

INDUSTRY STD

VAULTEDITIONS.COM

.DESIGNER.
DIETER STEFFMANN

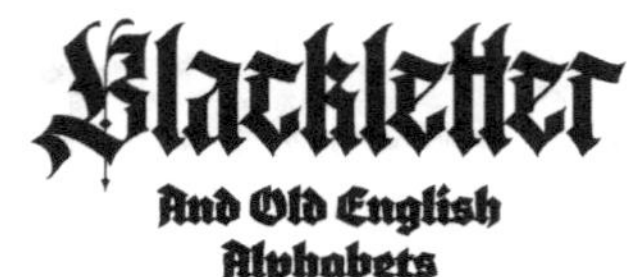
Blackletter
And Old English
Alphabets

.TYPEFACE.
WIEYNK FRAKTUR BOLD

UPPER | LOWER | NUMERALS ⟷ WEIGHT: BOLD ⟷ POINT SIZE: 82

ABCDEFGHIJKLM
NOPQRSTUVWXYZ
abcdefghijklmnopqrsstu
vwxyz
1234567890

Vault Editions Ltd  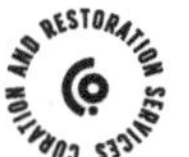 CURATION AND RESTORATION SERVICES

PRACTICE
MAKES
PERFECT

INDUSTRY STD

VAULTEDITIONS.COM

ABCDEFGHIJKLM
NOPQRSTUVWXYZ

abcdefghijklmnopqrstu
vwxyz

1234567890

29

ABCDEFGHIJKLMN
OPQRSTUVWXYZ
abcdefghijklmnopqrstu
vwxyz
1234567890

A HIGH RESOLUTION FILE OF THIS SPECIMEN SHEET CAN BE DOWNLOADED FROM THE VAULT EDITIONS' WEBSITE.

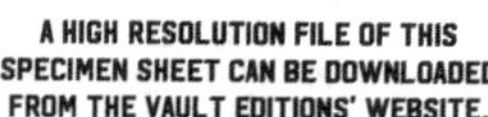
Vault Editions Ltd

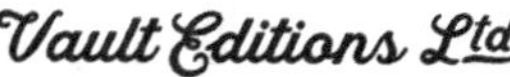

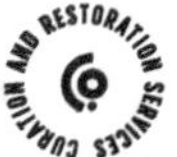
PRACTICE MAKES PERFECT

INDUSTRY STD

VAULTEDITIONS.COM

.DESIGNER.
DIETER STEFFMANN

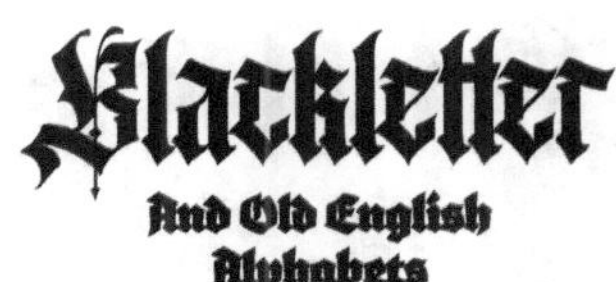

.TYPEFACE.
STEELPLATE TEXTURA

UPPER | LOWER | NUMERALS WEIGHT: REGULAR POINT SIZE: 80

A HIGH RESOLUTION FILE OF THIS SPECIMEN SHEET CAN BE DOWNLOADED FROM THE VAULT EDITIONS' WEBSITE.

Vault Editions Ltd

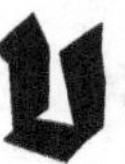

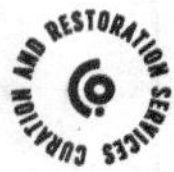

PRACTICE
MAKES
PERFECT
T·R·D   M·R·K

INDUSTRY STD

VAULTEDITIONS.COM

31

A HIGH RESOLUTION FILE OF THIS
SPECIMEN SHEET CAN BE DOWNLOADED
FROM THE VAULT EDITIONS' WEBSITE.

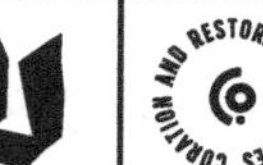

Vault Editions Ltd

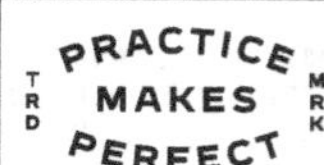

CURATION AND RESTORATION SERVICES

PRACTICE
MAKES
PERFECT

INDUSTRY STD

VAULTEDITIONS.COM

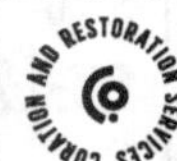

.DESIGNER.
DIETER STEFFMANN

Blackletter
And Old English Alphabets

.TYPEFACE.
PLAKAT FRAKTUR BLACK

UPPER | LOWER | NUMERALS ⟷ WEIGHT: REGULAR ⟷ POINT SIZE: 82

ABCDEFGHIJKLM
NOPQRSTUVWXYZ
abcdefghijklmnopqrst
uvwxyz
1234567890

Vault Editions Ltd

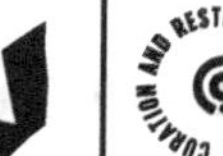

CURATION AND RESTORATION SERVICES · TRD

PRACTICE MAKES PERFECT · MRK

INDUSTRY STD

VAULTEDITIONS.COM

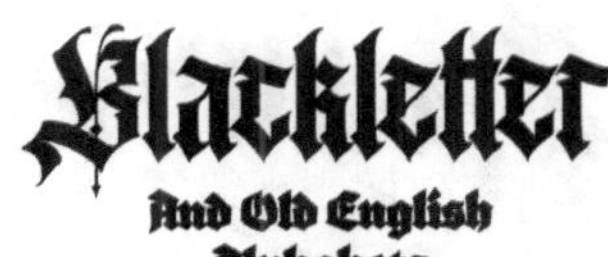

.TYPEFACE.
MODERNE FRAKTUR

34

ABCDEFGHIJKLM
NOPQRSTUVWXYZ
abcdefghijklmnopqr
stuvwxyz
1234567890

A HIGH RESOLUTION FILE OF THIS SPECIMEN SHEET CAN BE DOWNLOADED FROM THE VAULT EDITIONS' WEBSITE.

Vault Editions Ltd

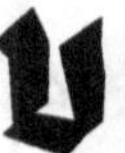

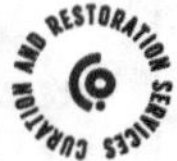

PRACTICE MAKES PERFECT

INDUSTRY STD

VAULTEDITIONS.COM

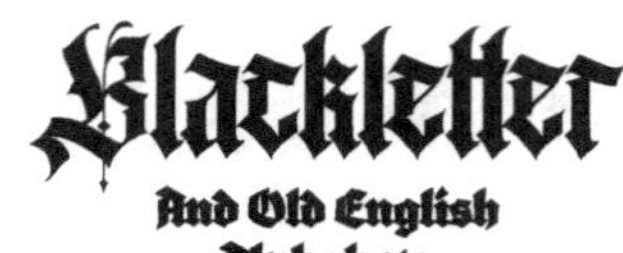

.TYPEFACE.
KABINETT FRAKTUR

UPPER | LOWER | NUMERALS ⟷ **WEIGHT: REGULAR** ⟷ **POINT SIZE: 81**

35

ABCDEFGHIJKLMN
OPQRSTUVWXYZ

abcdefghijklmnopqrstu
vwxyz

1234567890

Vault Editions Ltd

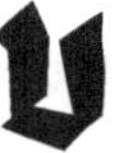
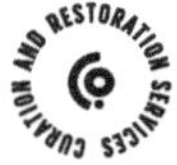

CURATION AND RESTORATION SERVICES

T·R·D PRACTICE MAKES PERFECT M·R·K

INDUSTRY STD

VAULTEDITIONS.COM

.DESIGNER.
DIETER STEFFMANN

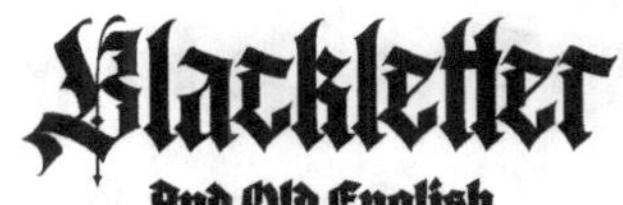

.TYPEFACE.
FRAKTUR SHOWED

UPPER | LOWER | NUMERALS   WEIGHT: REGULAR   POINT SIZE: 82

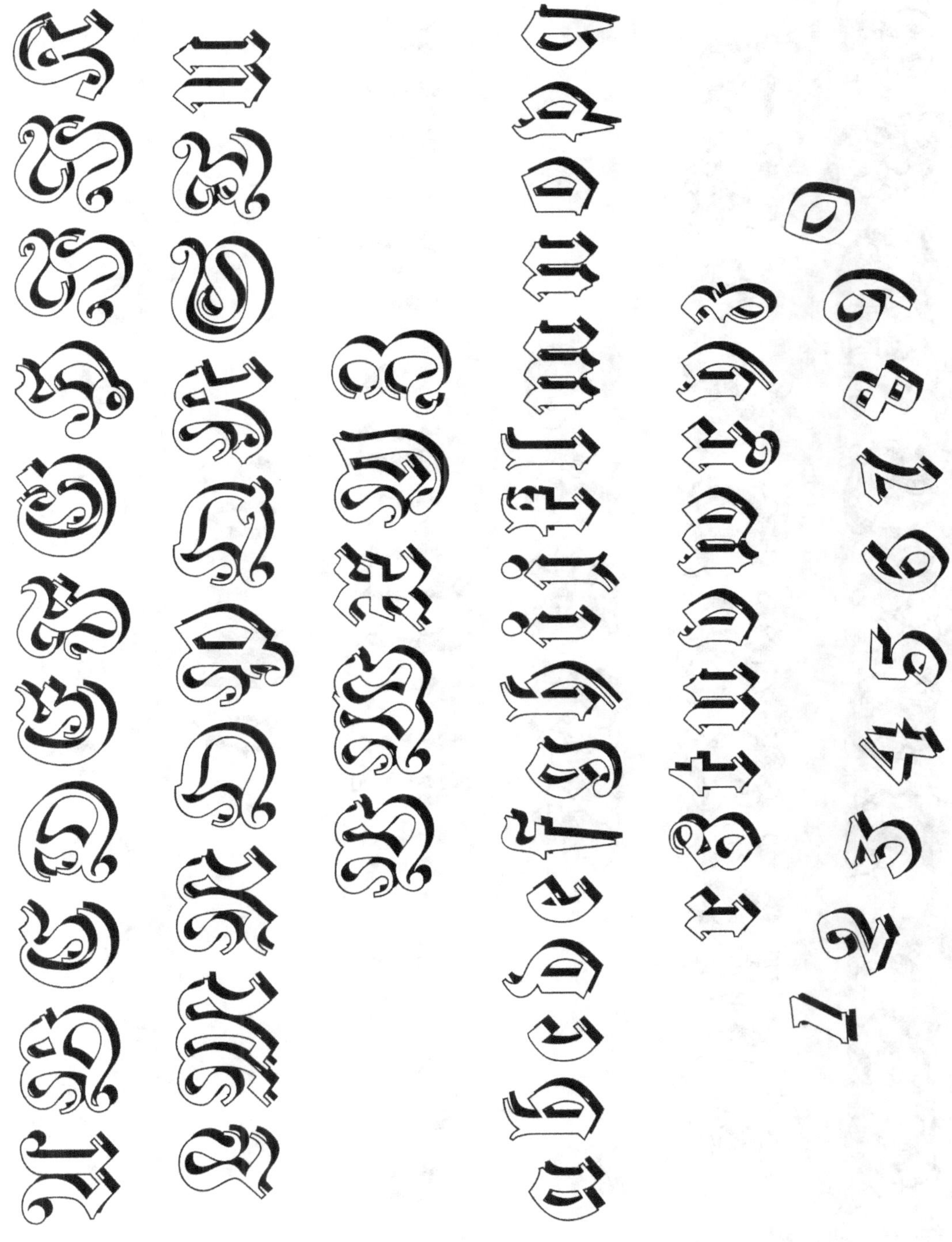

A HIGH RESOLUTION FILE OF THIS
SPECIMEN SHEET CAN BE DOWNLOADED
FROM THE VAULT EDITIONS' WEBSITE.

Vault Editions Ltd

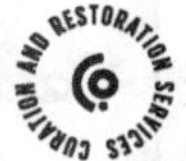

PRACTICE
MAKES
PERFECT
TRD MRK

INDUSTRY STD

VAULTEDITIONS.COM

.DESIGNER.
DIETER STEFFMANN

Blackletter
And Old English
Alphabets

.TYPEFACE.
**COELNISCHE CURRENT
FRAKTUR**

UPPER | LOWER | NUMERALS WEIGHT: REGULAR POINT SIZE: 83

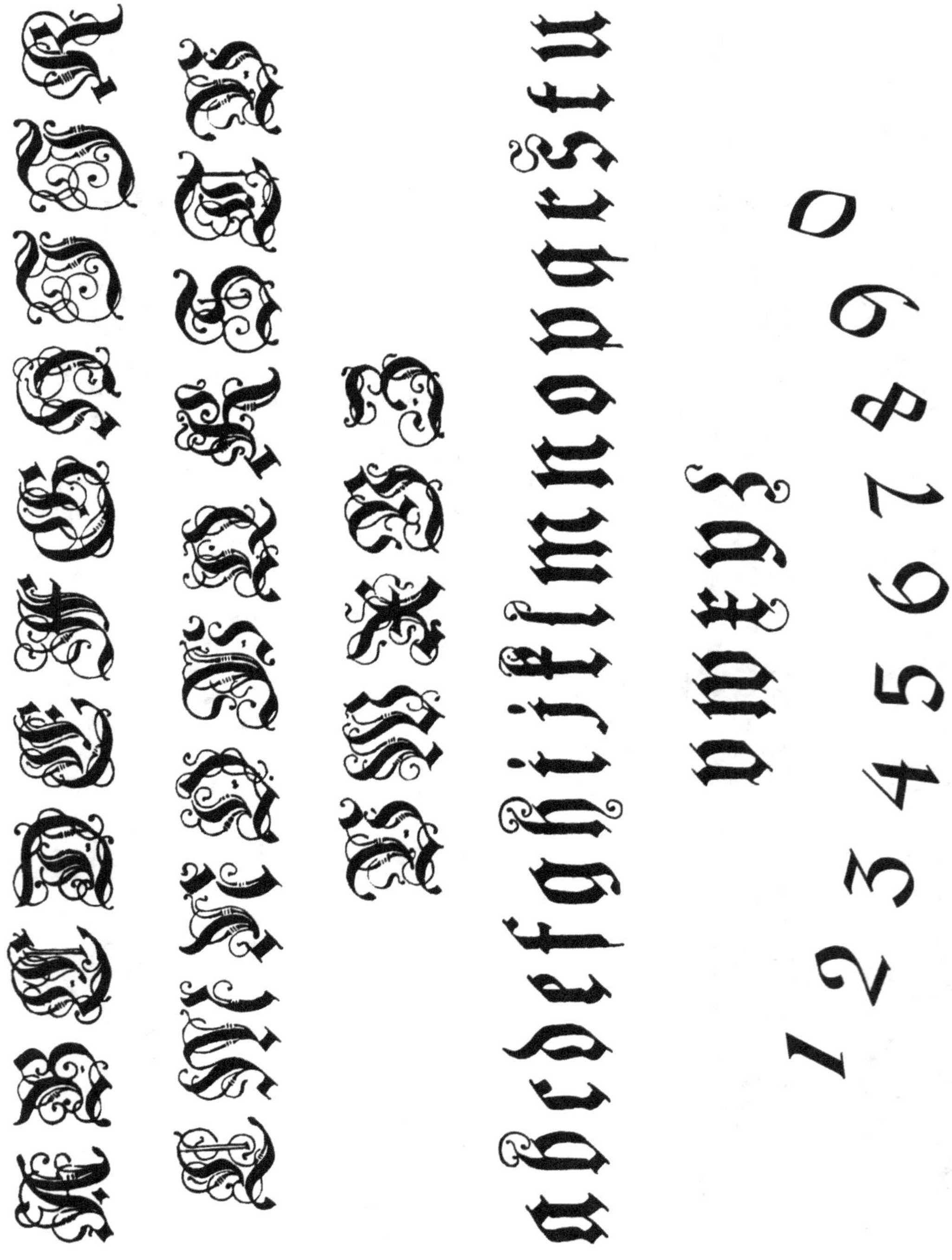

Vault Editions Ltd

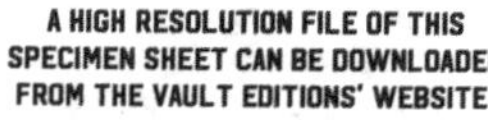
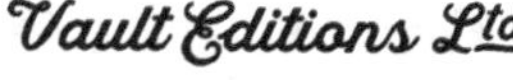

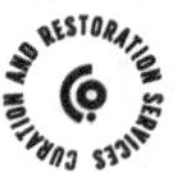

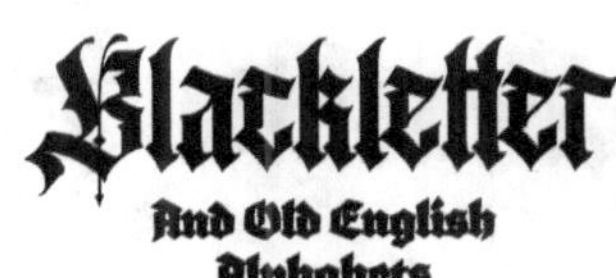

.TYPEFACE.

CHURSAECHSISCHE FRAKTUR

ABCDEFGHIJKLM
NOPQRSTUVWXYZ

abcdefghijklmnopqrstuvwxyz

1234567890

A HIGH RESOLUTION FILE OF THIS SPECIMEN SHEET CAN BE DOWNLOADED FROM THE VAULT EDITIONS' WEBSITE.

Vault Editions Ltd

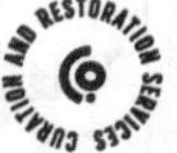

PRACTICE MAKES PERFECT

INDUSTRY STD

VAULTEDITIONS.COM

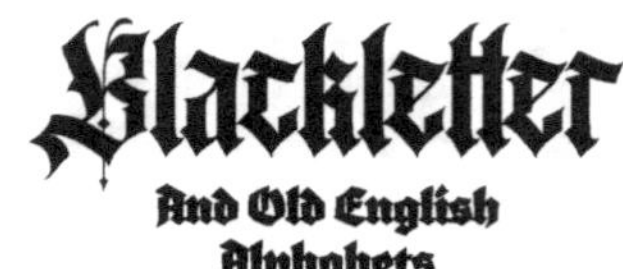

.TYPEFACE.
SCHAMPEL

UPPER | LOWER | NUMERALS   WEIGHT: REGULAR   POINT SIZE: 82

39

ABCDEFGHIJKLM
NOPQRSTUVWXYZ
abcdefghijklmnopqrstu
vwxyz
1234567890

Vault Editions Ltd

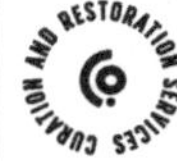
CURATION AND RESTORATION SERVICES

PRACTICE
MAKES
PERFECT
T R D · M R K

INDUSTRY STD

VAULTEDITIONS.COM

.DESIGNER.

DIETER STEFFMANN

Blackletter
And Old English
Alphabets

.TYPEFACE.

**ROTHENBURG
DECORATIVE**

UPPER | LOWER | NUMERALS ⟷ WEIGHT: REGULAR ⟷ POINT SIZE: 81

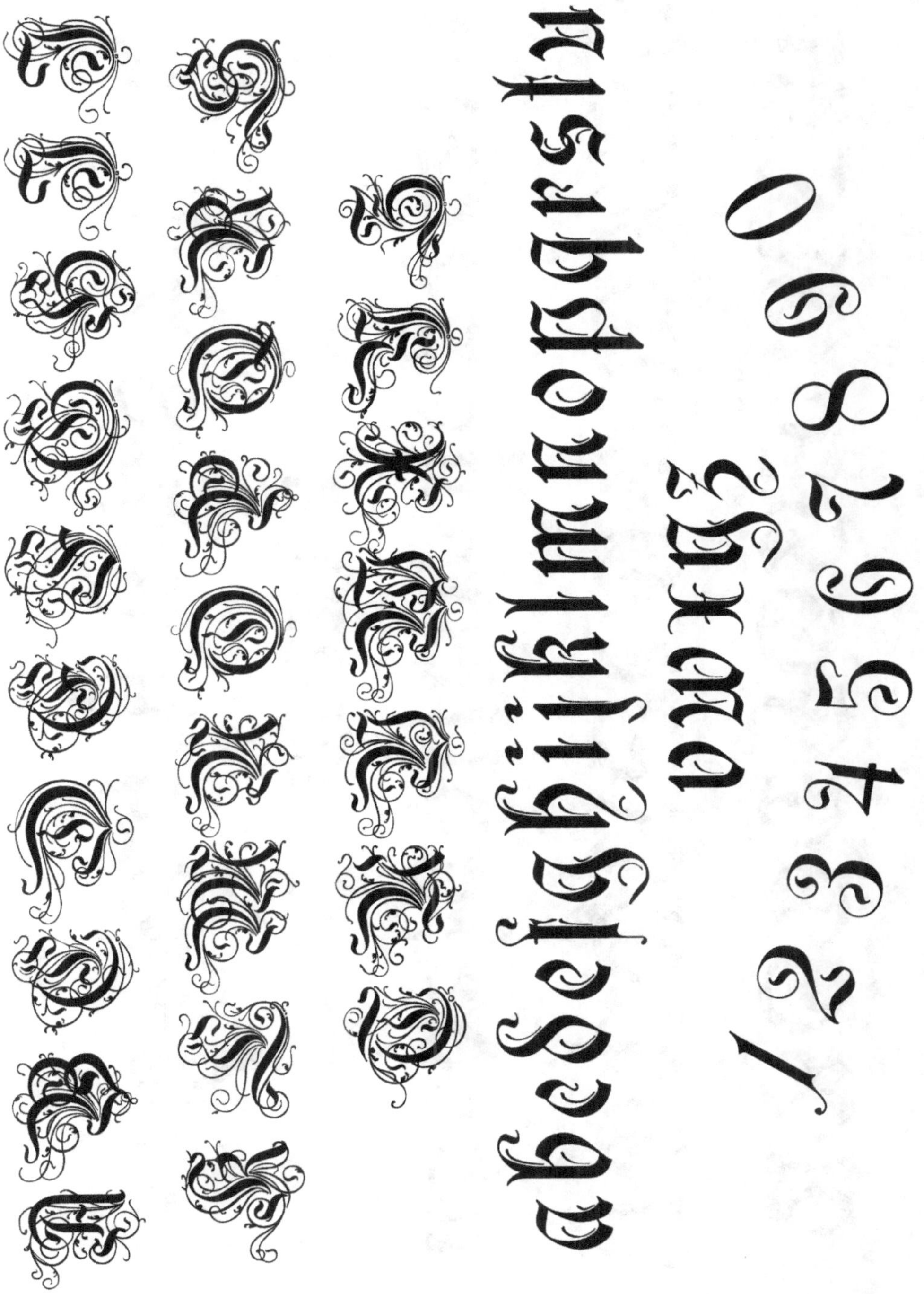

abcdefghijklmnopqrstu
vwxyz

1234567890

A HIGH RESOLUTION FILE OF THIS SPECIMEN SHEET CAN BE DOWNLOADED FROM THE VAULT EDITIONS' WEBSITE.

Vault Editions Ltd

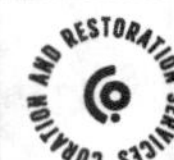

CURATION AND RESTORATION SERVICES

PRACTICE
MAKES
PERFECT
TRD MRK

INDUSTRY STD

VAULTEDITIONS.COM

41

ABCDEFGHIJKLMN
OPQRSTUVWXYZ
abcdefghijklmnopqrstu
vwxyz
1234567890

Vault Editions Ltd

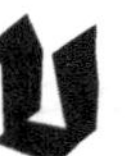
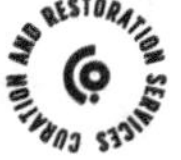

.DESIGNER.
DIETER STEFFMANN

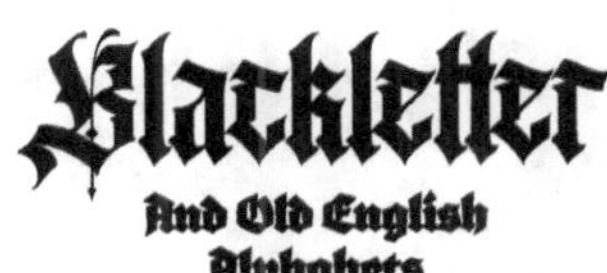

.TYPEFACE.
PROGRESSIVE TEXT

UPPER | LOWER | NUMERALS   WEIGHT: REGULAR   POINT SIZE: 80

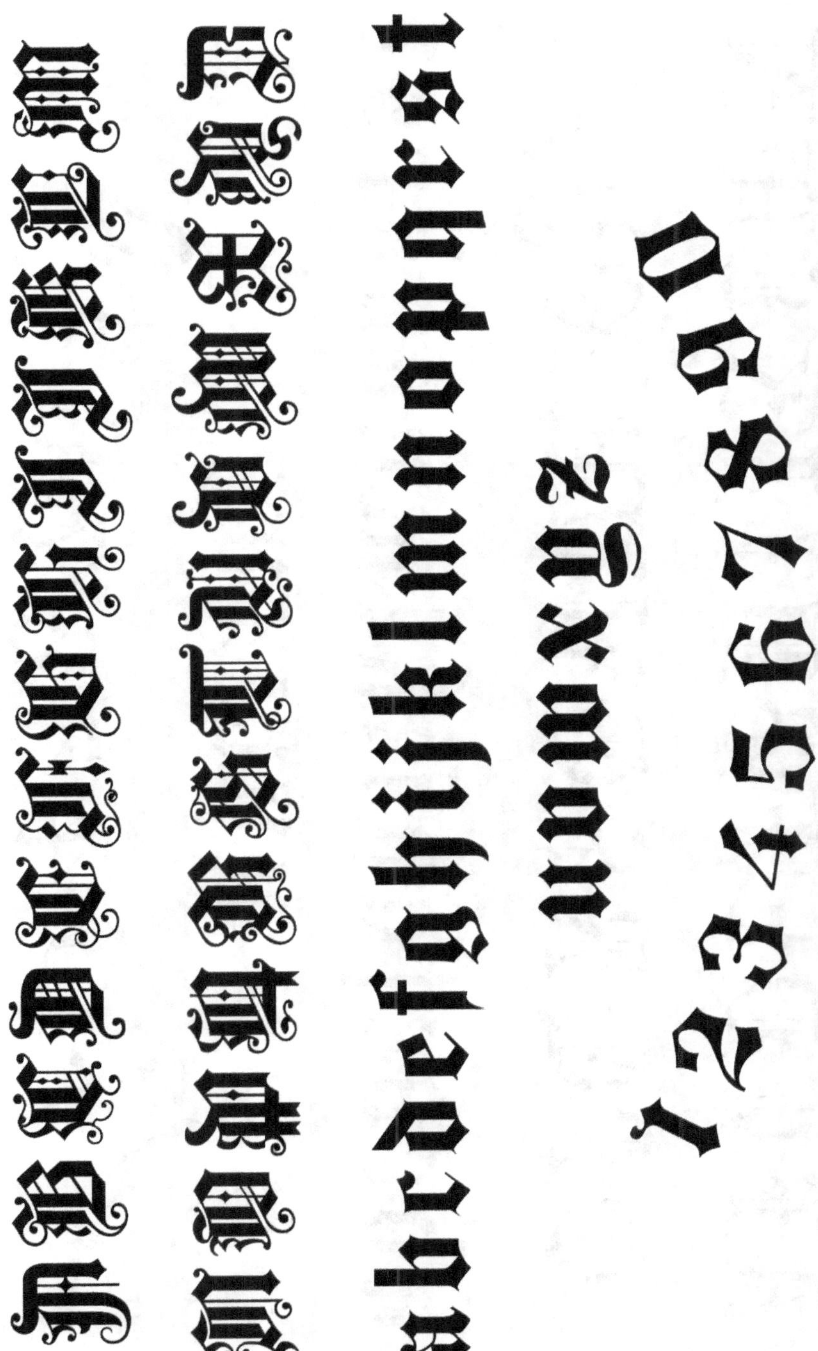

A HIGH RESOLUTION FILE OF THIS SPECIMEN SHEET CAN BE DOWNLOADED FROM THE VAULT EDITIONS' WEBSITE.

Vault Editions Ltd

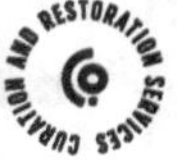

INDUSTRY STD

VAULTEDITIONS.COM

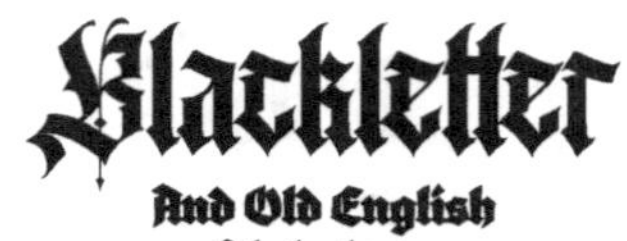

UPPER | LOWER | NUMERALS ←→ WEIGHT: REGULAR ←→ POINT SIZE: 82

43

ABCDEFGHIJKLMN
OPQRSTUVWXYZ
abcdefghijklmnopqrst
uvwxyz
1234567890

Vault Editions Ltd

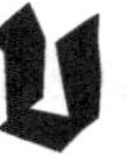

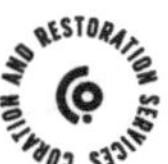

PRACTICE MAKES PERFECT
T R D · M R K

INDUSTRY STD

VAULTEDITIONS.COM

Blackletter
And Old English
Alphabets

44

ABCDEFGHIJKLMNOPQRSTUVWXYZ

abcdefghijklmnopqrstuvwxyz

1234567890

Vault Editions Ltd 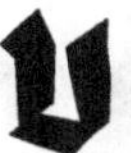 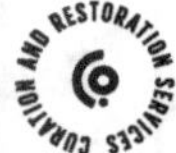

CURATION AND RESTORATION SERVICES

PRACTICE MAKES PERFECT

INDUSTRY STD

VAULTEDITIONS.COM

45

ABCDEFGHIJKLMN
OPQRSTUVWXYZ
abcdefghijklmnopqrs
tuvwxyz
1234567890

Vault Editions Ltd

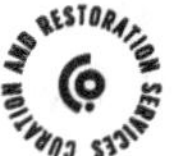

PRACTICE MAKES PERFECT

INDUSTRY STD

VAULTEDITIONS.COM

46

$$ABCDEFGHIJKLMN$$
$$OPQRSTUVWXYZ$$
$$abcdefghijklmnopqrst$$
$$uvwxyz$$
$$1234567890$$

Vault Editions Ltd

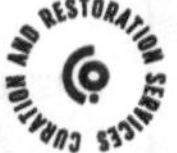

PRACTICE MAKES PERFECT

INDUSTRY STD

VAULTEDITIONS.COM

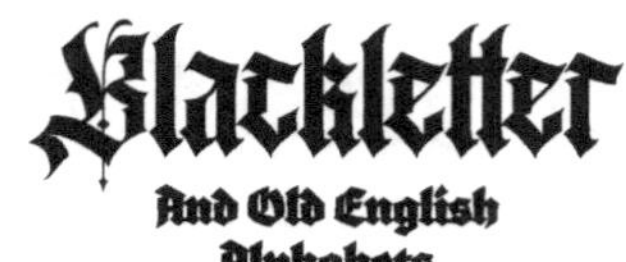

UPPER | LOWER | NUMERALS — WEIGHT: REGULAR — POINT SIZE: 82

47

A HIGH RESOLUTION FILE OF THIS SPECIMEN SHEET CAN BE DOWNLOADED FROM THE VAULT EDITIONS' WEBSITE.

Vault Editions Ltd

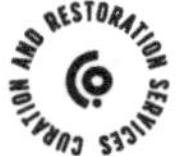

PRACTICE
MAKES
PERFECT
T R D · MRK

INDUSTRY STD

VAULTEDITIONS.COM

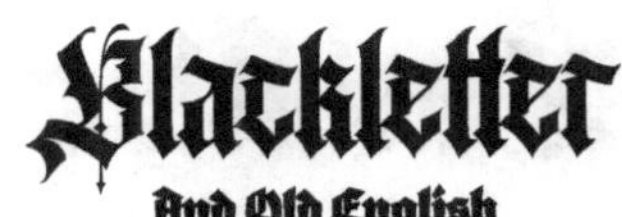

.TYPEFACE.
KOENIG TYPE
REGULAR

UPPER | LOWER | NUMERALS ⟷ WEIGHT: REGULAR ⟷ POINT SIZE: 82

48

ABCDEFGHIJKLM
NOPQRSTUVWXYZ
abcdefghijklmnopqrst
uvwxyz
1234567890

A HIGH RESOLUTION FILE OF THIS SPECIMEN SHEET CAN BE DOWNLOADED FROM THE VAULT EDITIONS' WEBSITE.

Vault Editions Ltd

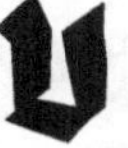

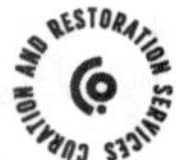

PRACTICE MAKES PERFECT

INDUSTRY STD
VAULTEDITIONS.COM

49

A B C D E F G H I J K L M
N O P Q R S T U V W X Y Z

a b c d e f g h i j k l m n o p q r s t
u v w x y z

0 1 2 3 4 5 6 7 8 9

Vault Editions Ltd

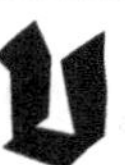

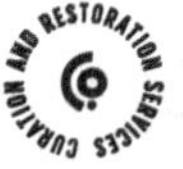

INDUSTRY STD

VAULTEDITIONS.COM

UPPER | LOWER | NUMERALS ⟷ WEIGHT: REGULAR ⟷ POINT SIZE: 81

50

ABCDEFGHIJKLMN
OPQRSTUVWXYZ
abcdefghijklmnopqrstu
vwxyz
1234567890

Vault Editions Ltd

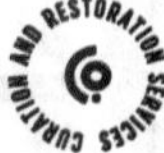

INDUSTRY STD

VAULTEDITIONS.COM

51

A B C D E F G H I J K L M N

O P Q R S T U V W X Y Z

a b c d e f g h i j k l m n o p q r s t

u v w x y z

0 6 8 2 9 5 4 3 2 1

Vault Editions Ltd

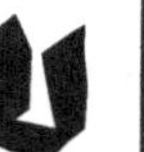

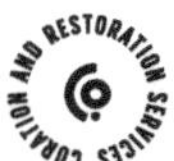

PRACTICE MAKES PERFECT

INDUSTRY STD

VAULTEDITIONS.COM

52

ABCDEFGHIJKLMNOPQRSTUVWXYZ

abcdefghijklmnopqrstuvwxyz

1234567890

Vault Editions Ltd

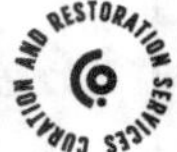

PRACTICE MAKES PERFECT

INDUSTRY STD

VAULTEDITIONS.COM

53

A B C D E F G H I J K L M
N O P Q R S T U V W X Y Z

a b c d e f g h i j k l m n o p q r s t
u v w x y z

1 2 3 4 5 6 7 8 9 0

Vault Editions Ltd

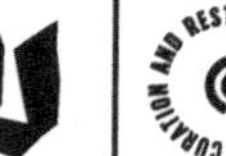 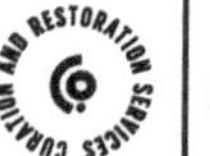

CURATION AND RESTORATION SERVICES

PRACTICE MAKES PERFECT

INDUSTRY STD

VAULTEDITIONS.COM

.DESIGNER.
DIETER STEFFMANN

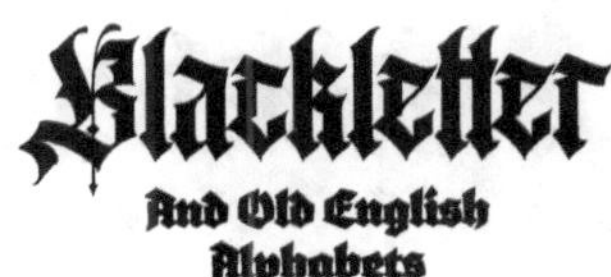

.TYPEFACE.
BLACK LETTER

UPPER | LOWER | NUMERALS ⟷ WEIGHT: REGULAR ⟷ POINT SIZE: 82

ABCDEFGHIJKLMN
OPQRSTUVWXYZ
abcdefghijklmnopqrst
uvwxyz
1234567890

A HIGH RESOLUTION FILE OF THIS SPECIMEN SHEET CAN BE DOWNLOADED FROM THE VAULT EDITIONS' WEBSITE.

Vault Editions Ltd

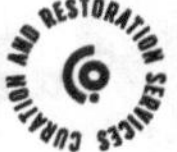

PRACTICE MAKES PERFECT
TRD MRK

INDUSTRY STD

VAULTEDITIONS.COM

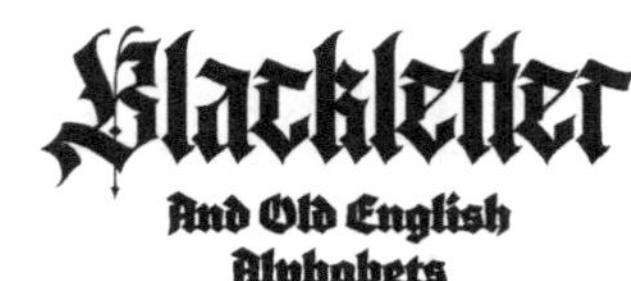

UPPER | LOWER | NUMERALS ⟷ WEIGHT: REGULAR ⟷ POINT SIZE: 81

55

ABCDEFGHIJKLM
NOPQRSTUVWXYZ

abcdefghijklmnopqrst
uvwxyz

1234567890

A HIGH RESOLUTION FILE OF THIS
SPECIMEN SHEET CAN BE DOWNLOADED
FROM THE VAULT EDITIONS' WEBSITE.

Vault Editions Ltd

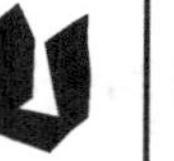
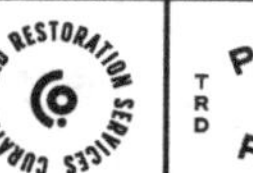

CURATION AND RESTORATION
SERVICES

PRACTICE
MAKES
PERFECT

INDUSTRY STD

VAULTEDITIONS.COM

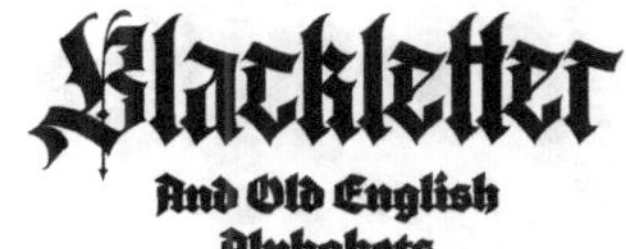

.TYPEFACE.
BECKETT KANZLEI

UPPER | LOWER | NUMERALS ⟷ WEIGHT: REGULAR ⟷ POINT SIZE: 82

A B C D E F G H I J K L M N O P Q R S T U V W X Y Z

a b c d e f g h i j k l m n o p q r s t u v w x y z

1 2 3 4 5 6 7 8 9 0

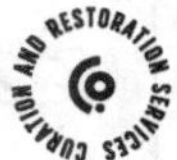

57

ABCDEFGHIJKLMNOP
QRSTUVWXYZ

abcdefghijklmnopqrstuv
wxyz

1234567890

Vault Editions Ltd

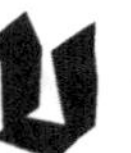
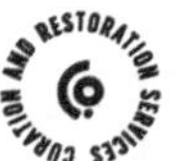

PRACTICE MAKES PERFECT

INDUSTRY STD

VAULTEDITIONS.COM

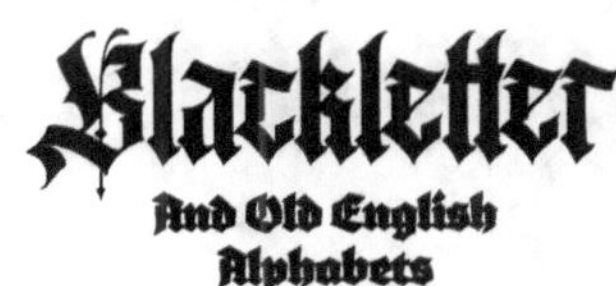

.TYPEFACE.
ALPINE

UPPER | LOWER | NUMERALS   WEIGHT: REGULAR   POINT SIZE: 81

58

ABCDEFGHIJKLMN
OPQRSTUVWXYZ

abcdefghijklmnopqrstu
vwxyz

1234567890

A HIGH RESOLUTION FILE OF THIS SPECIMEN SHEET CAN BE DOWNLOADED FROM THE VAULT EDITIONS' WEBSITE.

Vault Editions Ltd

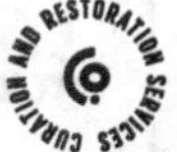

PRACTICE MAKES PERFECT

INDUSTRY STD

VAULTEDITIONS.COM

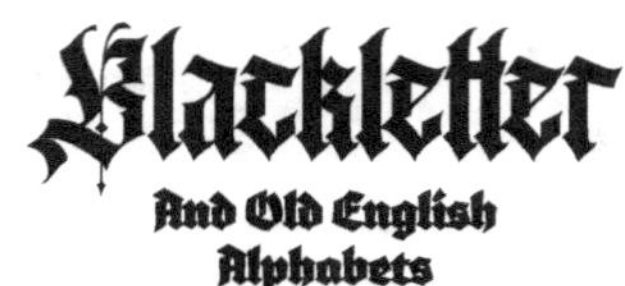

UPPER | LOWER | NUMERALS   ⟷   WEIGHT: REGULAR   ⟷   POINT SIZE: 83

59

ABCDEFGHIJKLM
NOPQRSTUVWXYZ
abcdefghijklmnopq
rstuvwxyz
1234567890

Vault Editions Ltd

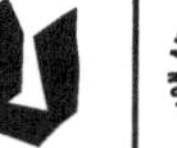
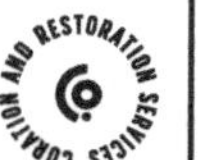
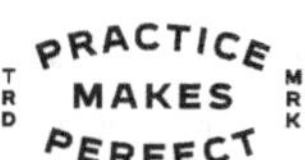

INDUSTRY STD
VAULTEDITIONS.COM

DIETER STEFFMANN

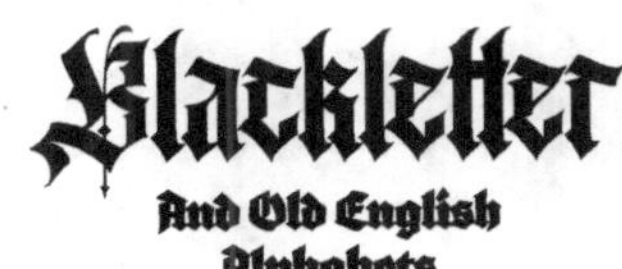

.TYPEFACE.

WEISS RUNDGOTISCH

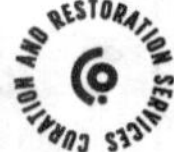

INDUSTRY STD

VAULTEDITIONS.COM

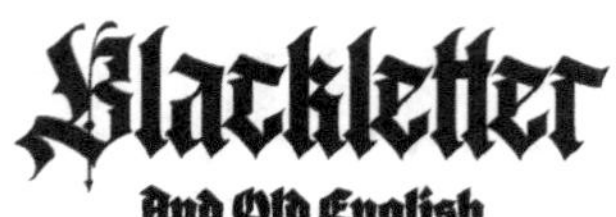

UPPER | LOWER | NUMERALS ⟷ WEIGHT: REGULAR ⟷ POINT SIZE: 82

61

𝕬𝕭𝕮𝕯𝕰𝕱𝕲𝕳𝕴𝕵𝕶𝕷𝕸

𝕹𝕺𝕻𝕼𝕽𝕾𝕿𝖀𝖁𝖂𝖃𝖄𝖅

abcdefghijklmnopqrstuv
wxyz

1 2 3 4 5 6 7 8 9 0

Vault Editions Ltd

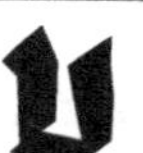

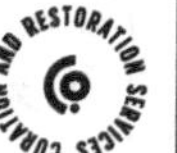

INDUSTRY STD

VAULTEDITIONS.COM

62

Vault Editions Ltd  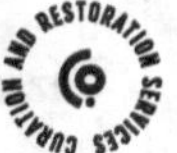

PRACTICE MAKES PERFECT

INDUSTRY STD

VAULTEDITIONS.COM

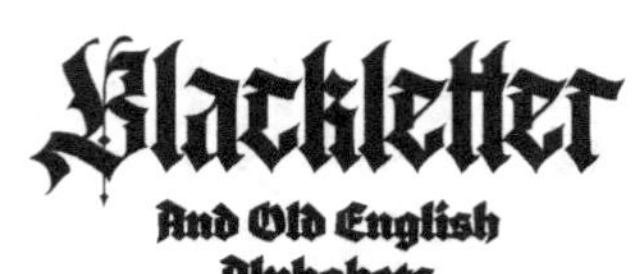

Blackletter
And Old English
Alphabets

·TYPEFACE·
TANNENBERG BOLD

UPPER | LOWER | NUMERALS ⟷ WEIGHT: REGULAR ⟷ POINT SIZE: 82

63

ABCDEFGHIJKLMN
OPQRSTUVWXYZ

abcdefghijklmnopqt
stuvwxyz

1234567890

A HIGH RESOLUTION FILE OF THIS SPECIMEN SHEET CAN BE DOWNLOADED FROM THE VAULT EDITIONS' WEBSITE.

Vault Editions Ltd

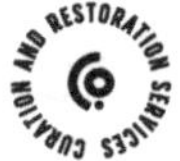

PRACTICE MAKES PERFECT

INDUSTRY STD

VAULTEDITIONS.COM

.DESIGNER.
DIETER STEFFMANN

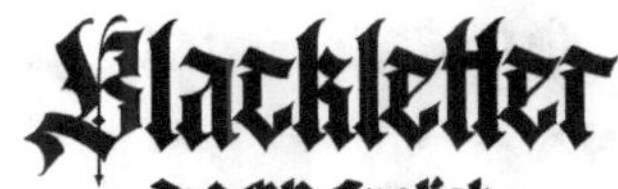
Blackletter
And Old English Alphabets

.TYPEFACE.
TANNENBERG SHADOW

UPPER | LOWER | NUMERALS ←→ WEIGHT: REGULAR ←→ POINT SIZE: 82

A HIGH RESOLUTION FILE OF THIS SPECIMEN SHEET CAN BE DOWNLOADED FROM THE VAULT EDITIONS' WEBSITE.

Vault Editions Ltd

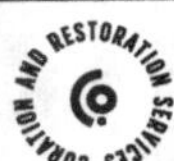

PRACTICE MAKES PERFECT
T R D   M R K

INDUSTRY STD

VAULTEDITIONS.COM

UPPER | LOWER | NUMERALS   ⟷   WEIGHT: REGULAR   ⟷   POINT SIZE: 82

65

Vault Editions Ltd

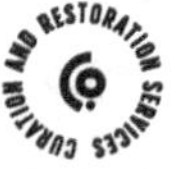

PRACTICE MAKES PERFECT

INDUSTRY STD

VAULTEDITIONS.COM

.DESIGNER.
DIETER STEFFMANN

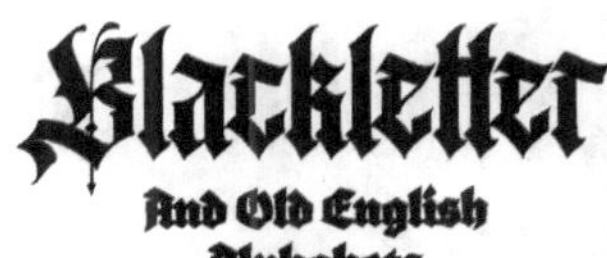

.TYPEFACE.
MIDDLE SAXONY TEXT

UPPER | LOWER | NUMERALS   WEIGHT: REGULAR   POINT SIZE: 82

ABCDEFGHIJKLM
NOPQRSTUVWXYZ
abcdefghijklmnopqrs
tuvwxyz
0 9 8 7 6 5 4 3 2 1

Vault Editions Ltd

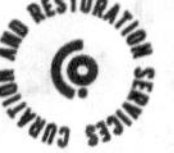

CURATION AND RESTORATION SERVICES CO

PRACTICE MAKES PERFECT
TRD MRK

INDUSTRY STD

VAULTEDITIONS.COM

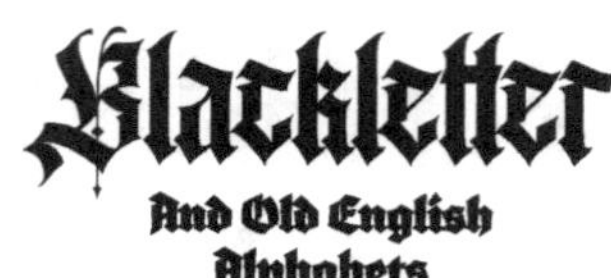

UPPER | LOWER | NUMERALS   ⟷   WEIGHT: REGULAR   ⟷   POINT SIZE: 82

Vault Editions Ltd

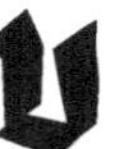
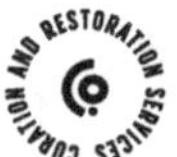

PRACTICE MAKES PERFECT

INDUSTRY STD

VAULTEDITIONS.COM

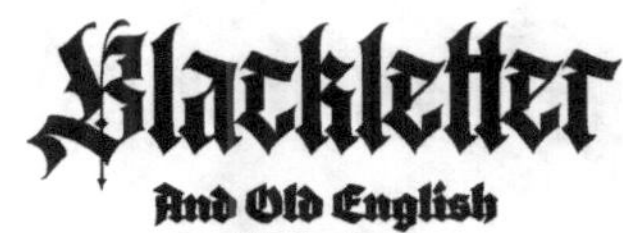

UPPER | LOWER | NUMERALS   WEIGHT: REGULAR   POINT SIZE: 81

68

A B C D E F G H I J K L M
N O P Q R S T U V W X Y Z
a b c d e f g h i j k l m n o p q r s t u
v w r y z
1 2 3 4 5 6 7 8 9 0

A HIGH RESOLUTION FILE OF THIS SPECIMEN SHEET CAN BE DOWNLOADED FROM THE VAULT EDITIONS' WEBSITE.

Vault Editions Ltd

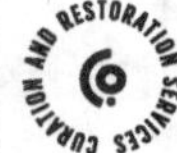

PRACTICE MAKES PERFECT

INDUSTRY STD

VAULTEDITIONS.COM

69

ABCDEFGHIJKLMNOPQRSTUVWXYZ

abcdefghijklmnopqrstuvwxyz

1234567890

Vault Editions Ltd

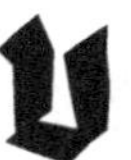

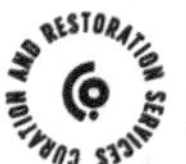

INDUSTRY STD

VAULTEDITIONS.COM

70

Vault Editions Ltd

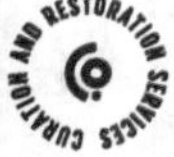

PRACTICE
TRD MAKES MRK
PERFECT

INDUSTRY STD

VAULTEDITIONS.COM

.DESIGNER.
DIETER STEFFMANN

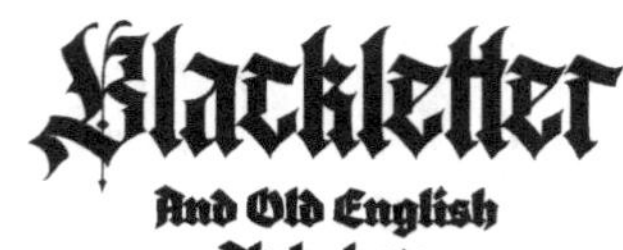

.TYPEFACE.
HUMBOLDT FRAKTUR
ZIERBUCHSTABEN

UPPER | LOWER | NUMERALS ⟷ WEIGHT: REGULAR ⟷ POINT SIZE: 80

𝔄𝔅ℭ𝔇𝔈𝔉𝔊ℌℑ𝔍𝔎𝔏𝔐
𝔑𝔒𝔓𝔔ℜ𝔖𝔗𝔘𝔙𝔚𝔛𝔜ℨ
𝔞𝔟𝔠𝔡𝔢𝔣𝔤𝔥𝔦𝔧𝔨𝔩𝔪𝔫𝔬𝔭𝔮𝔯𝔰𝔱𝔲
𝔳𝔴𝔵𝔶𝔷

1 2 3 4 5 6 7 8 9 0

Vault Editions Ltd

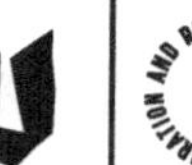

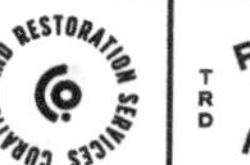

PRACTICE MAKES PERFECT
TRD MRK

INDUSTRY STD

VAULTEDITIONS.COM

.DESIGNER.
DIETER STEFFMANN

Blackletter
And Old English
Alphabets

.TYPEFACE.
GUTENBERG TEXTURA

UPPER | LOWER | NUMERALS ⟷ WEIGHT: REGULAR ⟷ POINT SIZE: 83

ABCDEFFGHIJKLM
NOPQRSTUVWXYZ
abcdefghijklmnopqrstu
vwxyz
1234567890

A HIGH RESOLUTION FILE OF THIS SPECIMEN SHEET CAN BE DOWNLOADED FROM THE VAULT EDITIONS' WEBSITE.

Vault Editions Ltd

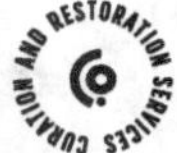

CURATION AND RESTORATION SERVICES CO

PRACTICE MAKES PERFECT
TRD · MRK

INDUSTRY STD

VAULTEDITIONS.COM

73

ABCDEFGGHIJKLMN
OPQRSTUVWXYZ
abcdefghiiklmnopqrstu
vwxyz
1234567890

.DESIGNER.
DIETER STEFFMANN

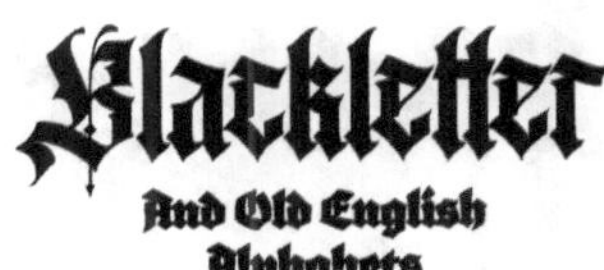

.TYPEFACE.
FETTE HAENEL FRAKTUR

UPPER | LOWER | NUMERALS WEIGHT: REGULAR POINT SIZE: 82

A HIGH RESOLUTION FILE OF THIS SPECIMEN SHEET CAN BE DOWNLOADED FROM THE VAULT EDITIONS' WEBSITE.

Vault Editions Ltd

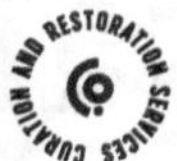

PRACTICE MAKES PERFECT

INDUSTRY STD

VAULTEDITIONS.COM

75

ABCDEFGHIJKLMN
OPQRSTUVWXYZ
abcdefghijklmnopqrst
uvwxyz
1234567890

Vault Editions Ltd

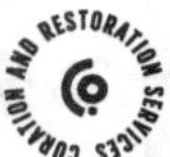

CURATION AND RESTORATION SERVICES

PRACTICE MAKES PERFECT

INDUSTRY STD

VAULTEDITIONS.COM

.DESIGNER.
DIETER STEFFMANN

Blackletter
And Old English Alphabets

.TYPEFACE.
DS ZIERSCHRIFT

UPPER | LOWER | NUMERALS ⟷ WEIGHT: REGULAR ⟷ POINT SIZE: 83

.DESIGNER.
DIETER STEFFMANN

Blackletter
And Old English
Alphabets

.TYPEFACE.
DS WALLAU

UPPER | LOWER | NUMERALS ⟷ WEIGHT: REGULAR ⟷ POINT SIZE: 82

ABCDEFGHIJKLMN
OPQRSTUVWXYZ
abcdefghijklmnopq
rstuvwxyz
1234567890

A HIGH RESOLUTION FILE OF THIS SPECIMEN SHEET CAN BE DOWNLOADED FROM THE VAULT EDITIONS' WEBSITE.

Vault Editions Ltd

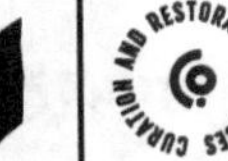

PRACTICE MAKES PERFECT

INDUSTRY STD

VAULTEDITIONS.COM

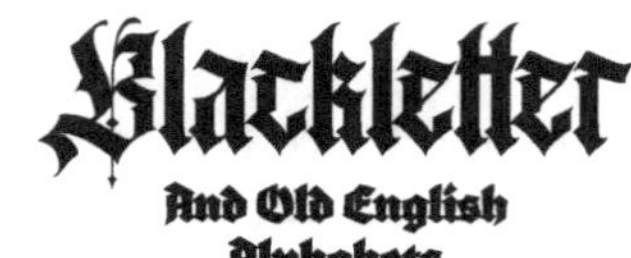

.DESIGNER.
DIETER STEFFMANN

.TYPEFACE.
**DS WALBAUM
FRAKTUR**

UPPER | LOWER | NUMERALS ⟷ WEIGHT: REGULAR ⟷ POINT SIZE: 83

A HIGH RESOLUTION FILE OF THIS SPECIMEN SHEET CAN BE DOWNLOADED FROM THE VAULT EDITIONS' WEBSITE.

Vault Editions Ltd

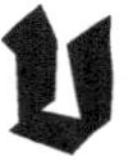

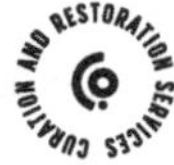

PRACTICE MAKES PERFECT

INDUSTRY STD

VAULTEDITIONS.COM

ABCDEFGHIJKLM
NOPQRSTUVWXYZ
abcdefghijklmnopqrstu
vwxyz
1234567890

UPPER | LOWER | NUMERALS   WEIGHT: REGULAR   POINT SIZE: 83

81

ABCDEFGHIJKLM
NOPQRSTUVWXYZ
abcdefghijklmnopqrstu
vwxyz
1234567890

Vault Editions Ltd

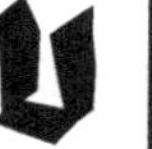
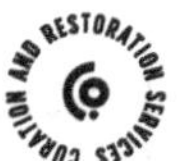

PRACTICE MAKES PERFECT

INDUSTRY STD

VAULTEDITIONS.COM

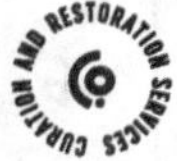

83

Vault Editions Ltd

CURATION AND RESTORATION SERVICES

TRD PRACTICE MAKES PERFECT MRK

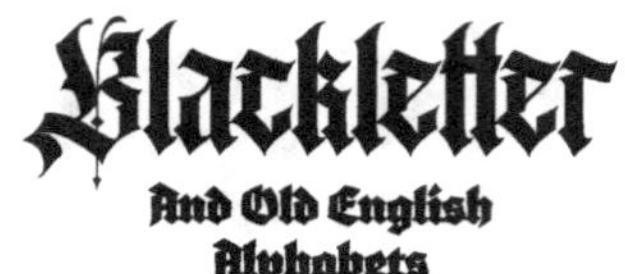

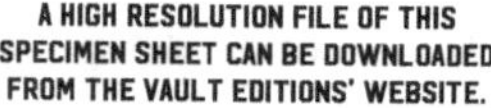

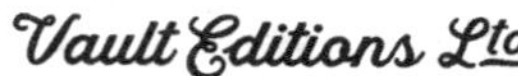

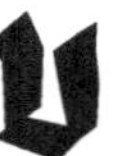

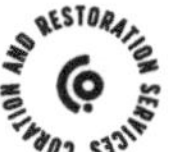

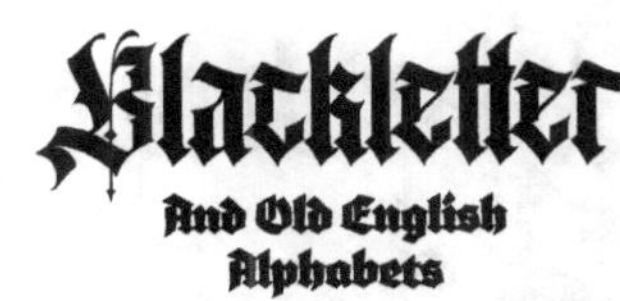

.TYPEFACE.
DS BALLADE

UPPER | LOWER | NUMERALS ⟷ WEIGHT: REGULAR ⟷ POINT SIZE: 83

84

A HIGH RESOLUTION FILE OF THIS SPECIMEN SHEET CAN BE DOWNLOADED FROM THE VAULT EDITIONS' WEBSITE.

Vault Editions Ltd

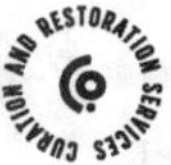

PRACTICE
MAKES
PERFECT
T R D   M R K

INDUSTRY STD

VAULTEDITIONS.COM

UPPER | LOWER | NUMERALS ⟷ WEIGHT: REGULAR ⟷ POINT SIZE: 83

85

Vault Editions Ltd

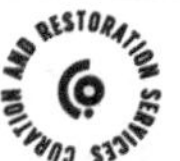

PRACTICE
MAKES
PERFECT

INDUSTRY STD

VAULTEDITIONS.COM

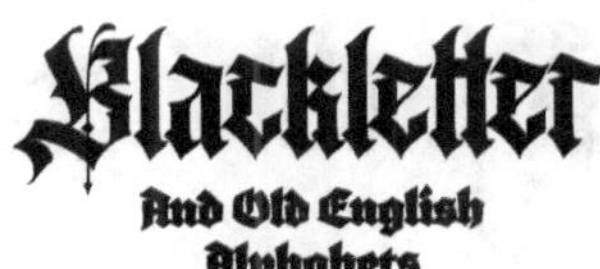

ABCDEFGHIJKLMN
OPQRSTUVWXYZ
abcdefghijklmnopqrstu
vwxyz
1234567890

A HIGH RESOLUTION FILE OF THIS SPECIMEN SHEET CAN BE DOWNLOADED FROM THE VAULT EDITIONS' WEBSITE.

Vault Editions Ltd

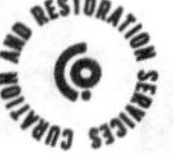

PRACTICE MAKES PERFECT

INDUSTRY STD

VAULTEDITIONS.COM

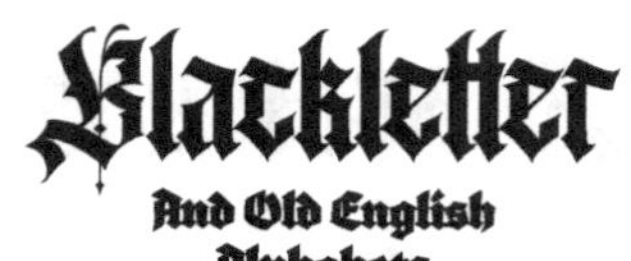

.TYPEFACE.
BREITKOPF FRAKTUR

UPPER | LOWER | NUMERALS ⟷ WEIGHT: REGULAR ⟷ POINT SIZE: 81

ABCDEFGHIJKLM
NOPQRSTUVWXYZ
abcdefghijklmnopqrstu
vwxyz
1234567890

.DESIGNER.
DIETER STEFFMANN

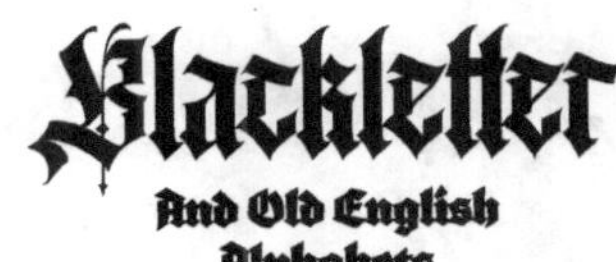

.TYPEFACE.
ALTE SCHWABACHER

UPPER | LOWER | NUMERALS ⟷ WEIGHT: REGULAR ⟷ POINT SIZE: 82

ABCDEFGHIJKLM
NOPQRSTUVWXYZ
abcdefghijflmnopqrstuv
wxyz
1234567890

Vault Editions Ltd

CURATION AND RESTORATION SERVICES · TRD ©

PRACTICE MAKES PERFECT · TRD · MRK

INDUSTRY STD

VAULTEDITIONS.COM

UPPER | LOWER | NUMERALS   ⟷   WEIGHT: REGULAR   ⟷   POINT SIZE: 83

89

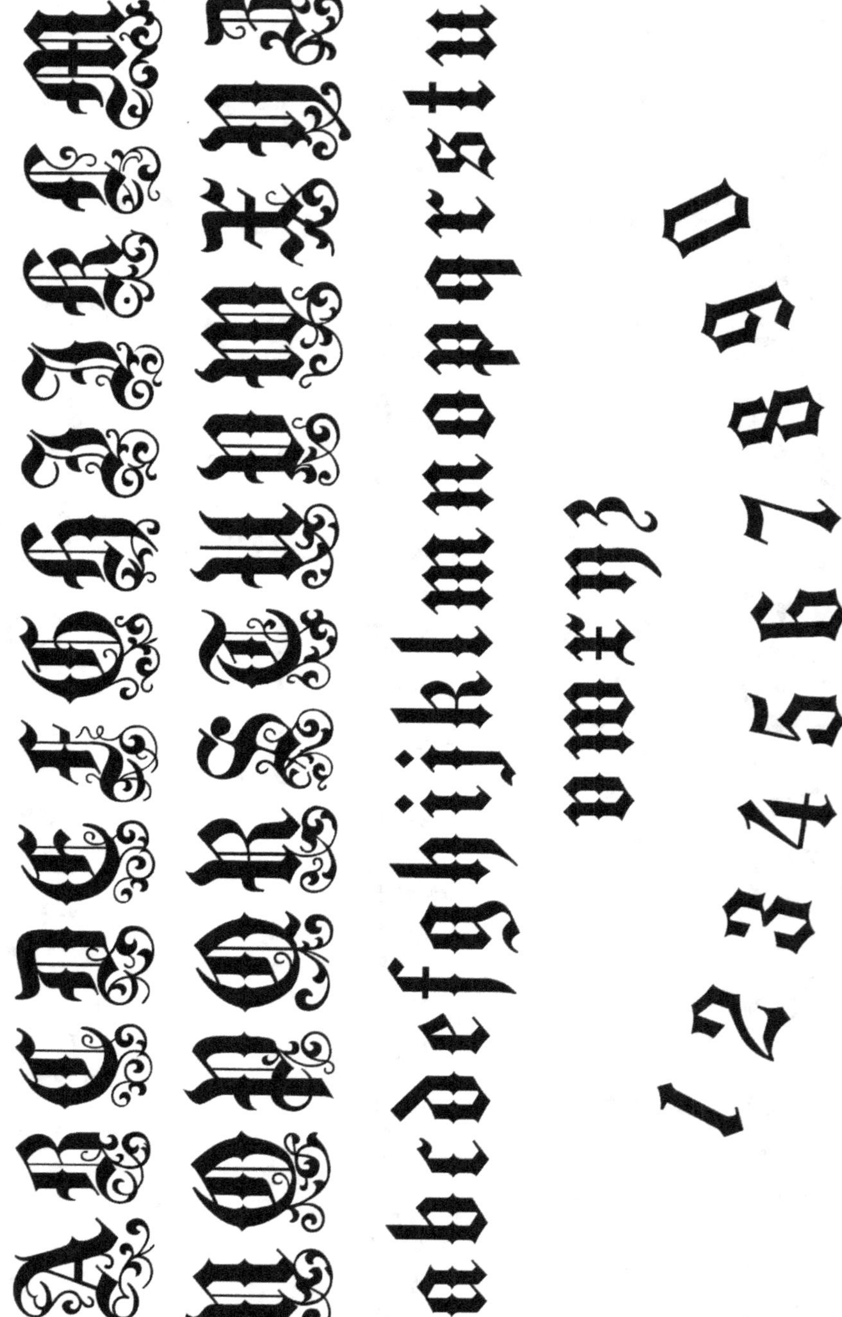

Vault Editions Ltd

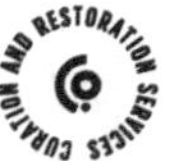

PRACTICE MAKES PERFECT

INDUSTRY STD

VAULTEDITIONS.COM

.DESIGNER.
PETER WIEGEL

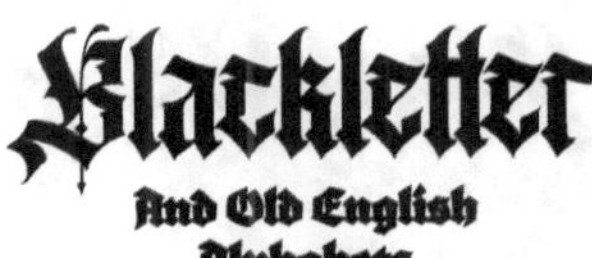
Blackletter
And Old English
Alphabets

.TYPEFACE.
**WERNICKE
SCHWABACHER**

UPPER | LOWER | NUMERALS ⟷ WEIGHT: REGULAR ⟷ POINT SIZE: 83

ABCDEFGHIJKLMNO
PQRSTUVWXYZ

abcdefghijklmnopqrstuv
wxyz

1234567890

Vault Editions Ltd

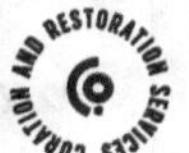

CURATION AND RESTORATION SERVICES

PRACTICE MAKES PERFECT

INDUSTRY STD

VAULTEDITIONS.COM

UPPER | LOWER | NUMERALS ⟷ WEIGHT: REGULAR ⟷ POINT SIZE: 83

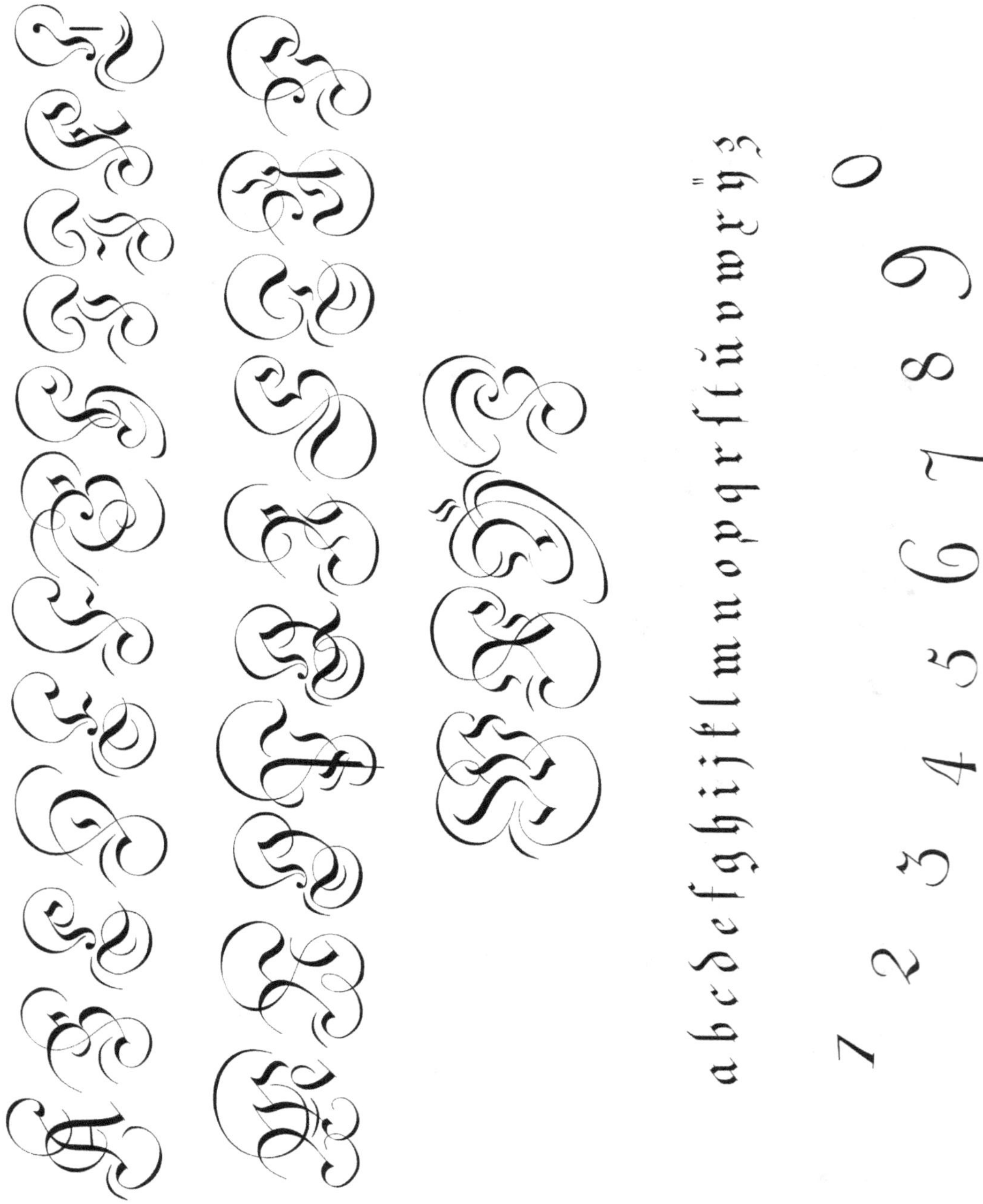

91

a b c d e f g h i j k l m n o p q r f t u v w r y z

1 2 3 4 5 6 7 8 9 0

Vault Editions Ltd

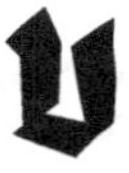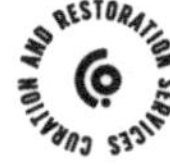

PRACTICE MAKES PERFECT

INDUSTRY STD

VAULTEDITIONS.COM

.DESIGNER.
PETER WIEGEL

Blackletter
And Old English
Alphabets

.TYPEFACE.
RENATA CAT

UPPER | LOWER | NUMERALS ⟷ WEIGHT: REGULAR ⟷ POINT SIZE: 83

ABCDEFGHIJKL
MNOPQRSTUV
WXYZ
abcdefghiijkllmnopqrst
uvwxyz
1234567890

Vault Editions Ltd

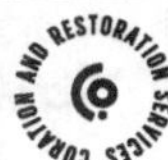

CURATION AND RESTORATION SERVICES

PRACTICE MAKES PERFECT
TRD MRK

INDUSTRY STD

VAULTEDITIONS.COM

UPPER | LOWER | NUMERALS ⟷ WEIGHT: REGULAR ⟷ POINT SIZE: 83

93

ABCDEFGHIJKL
MNOPQRSTUVW
+ XYZ +
abcdefghijklmnopqrstu
vwxyz
1234567890

Vault Editions Ltd

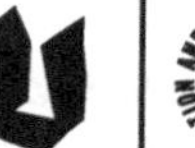
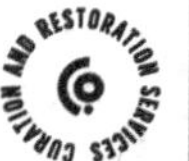

CURATION AND RESTORATION SERVICES

PRACTICE MAKES PERFECT
TRD MRK

INDUSTRY STD

VAULTEDITIONS.COM

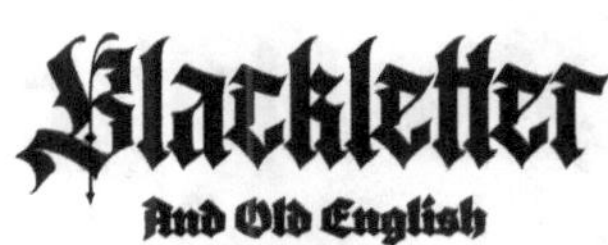

Blackletter
And Old English
Alphabets

UPPER | LOWER | NUMERALS ⟷ WEIGHT: REGULAR ⟷ POINT SIZE: 83

ABCDEFGHIJK
LMNOPQRSTUVW
XYZ

abcdefghijklmnopqrs
tuvwxyz

1234567890

Vault Editions Ltd

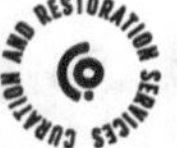

PRACTICE
MAKES
PERFECT

INDUSTRY STD

VAULTEDITIONS.COM

.DESIGNER.
PETER WIEGEL

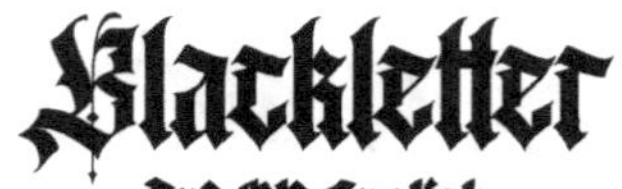

.TYPEFACE.
NEUE ZIER SCHRIFT

UPPER | LOWER | NUMERALS ⟷ WEIGHT: REGULAR ⟷ POINT SIZE: 82

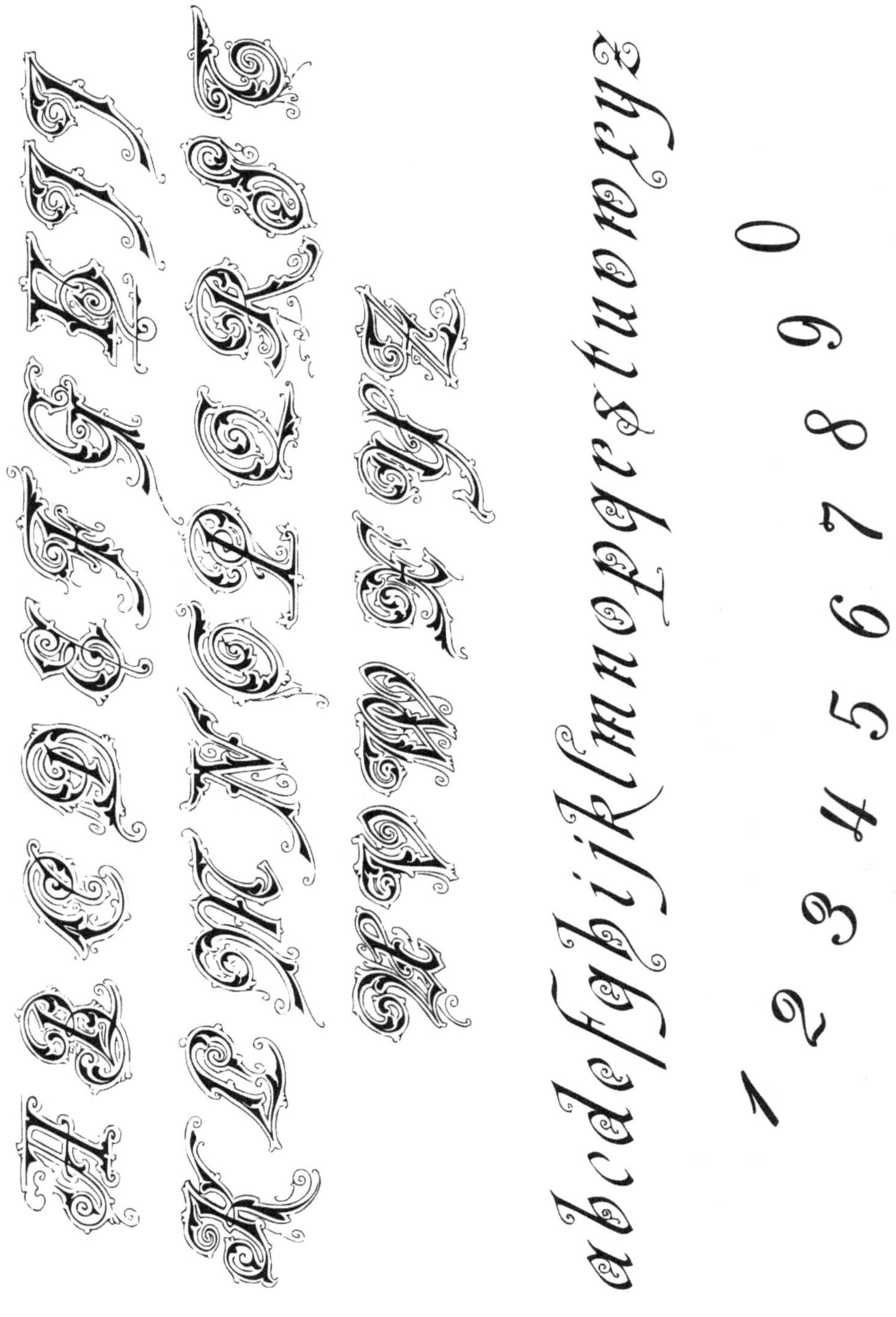

abcdefghijklmnopqrstuvwxyz
1 2 3 4 5 6 7 8 9 0

Vault Editions Ltd

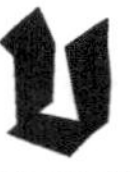

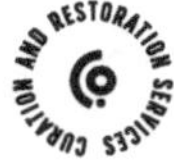

PRACTICE
MAKES
PERFECT
T R D — M R K

INDUSTRY STD

VAULTEDITIONS.COM

UPPER | LOWER | NUMERALS ⟷   WEIGHT: BOLD ⟷   POINT SIZE: 83

ABCDEFGHIJKL
MNOPQRSTU
VWXYZ

abcdefghijklmnopqrstu
vwxyz

1234567890

Vault Editions Ltd

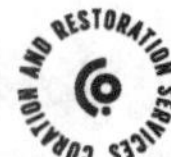

PRACTICE MAKES PERFECT

INDUSTRY STD

VAULTEDITIONS.COM

97

ABCDEFGHIJKL
MNOPQRSTUVW
XYZ

abcdefghijklmnopqrs
tuvwxyz

1234567890

Vault Editions Ltd

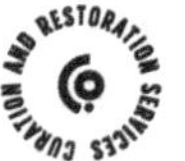

PRACTICE
MAKES
PERFECT
TRD MRK

INDUSTRY STD

VAULTEDITIONS.COM

UPPER | LOWER | NUMERALS — WEIGHT: REGULAR — POINT SIZE: 83

ABCDEFGHIJKLMNOPQRSTUVWXYZ

abcdefghijklmnopqrstuvwxyz

1234567890

Vault Editions Ltd

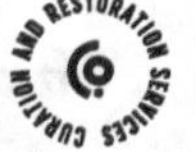

INDUSTRY STD

VAULTEDITIONS.COM

99

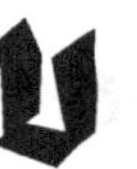
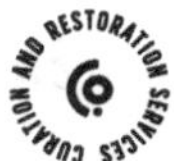

.DESIGNER.
PETER WIEGEL

Blackletter
And Old English
Alphabets

.TYPEFACE.
JENA GOTISCH

UPPER | LOWER | NUMERALS ⟷   WEIGHT: REGULAR   ⟷   POINT SIZE: 83

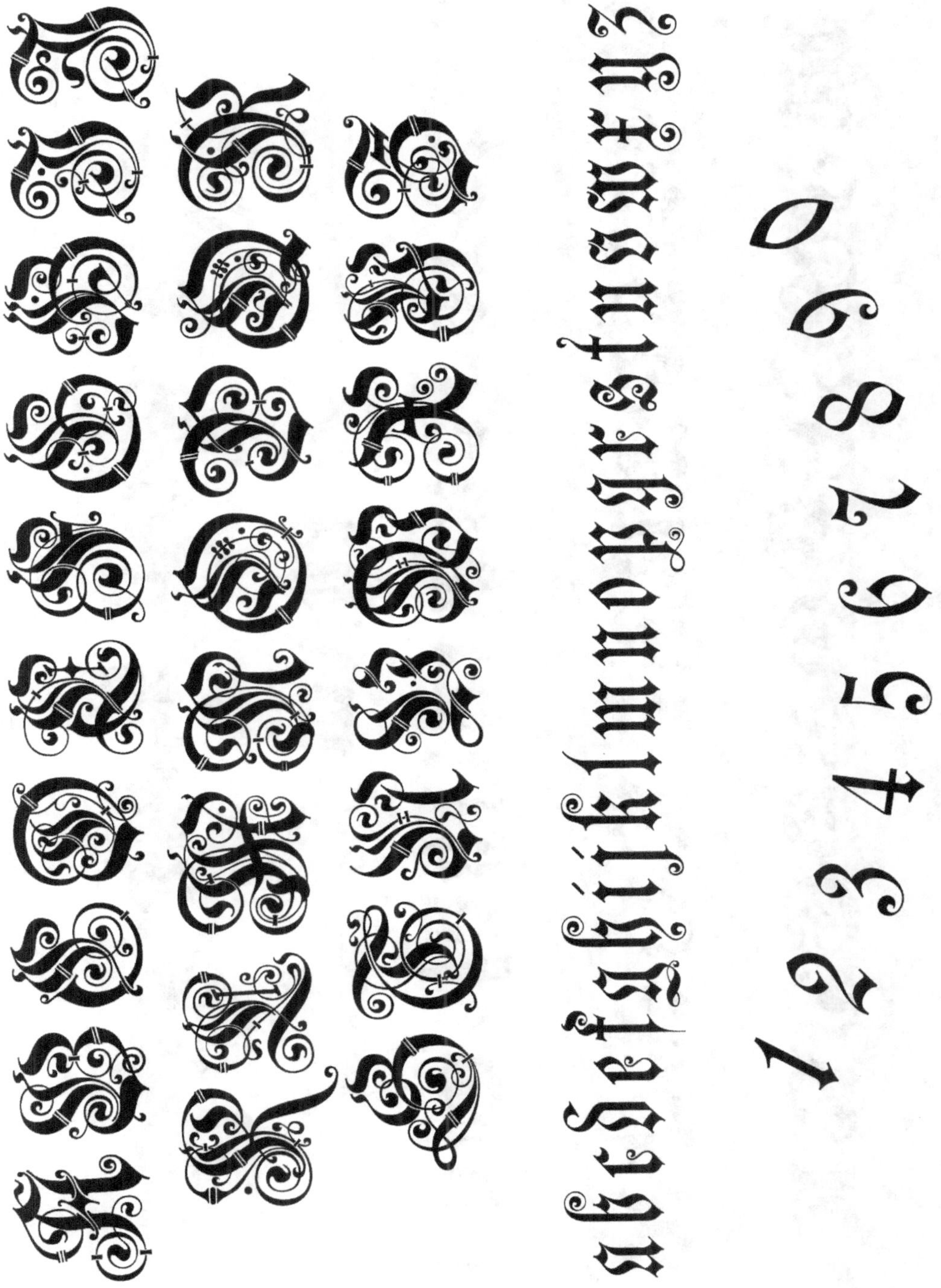

A HIGH RESOLUTION FILE OF THIS SPECIMEN SHEET CAN BE DOWNLOADED FROM THE VAULT EDITIONS' WEBSITE.

Vault Editions Ltd

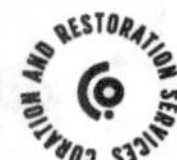

PRACTICE
MAKES
PERFECT

INDUSTRY STD

VAULTEDITIONS.COM

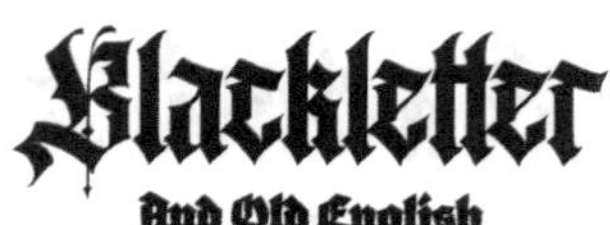

.TYPEFACE.
FETTE NATIONAL
FRAKTUR

UPPER | LOWER | NUMERALS   ⟷   WEIGHT: REGULAR   ⟷   POINT SIZE: 81

101

A HIGH RESOLUTION FILE OF THIS
SPECIMEN SHEET CAN BE DOWNLOADED
FROM THE VAULT EDITIONS' WEBSITE.

Vault Editions Ltd

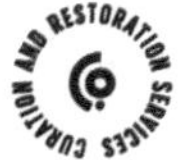

PRACTICE
T R D   MAKES   MRK
PERFECT

INDUSTRY STD

VAULTEDITIONS.COM

.DESIGNER.

PETER WIEGEL

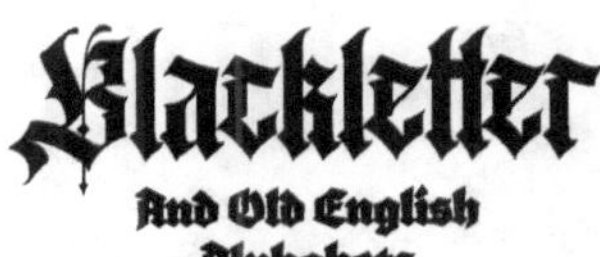

Blackletter
And Old English
Alphabets

.TYPEFACE.

EHMCKE FEDERFRAKTUR

UPPER | LOWER | NUMERALS WEIGHT: REGULAR POINT SIZE: 81

ABCDEFGHJKLM
NOPQRSTUVWXYZ

abcdefghijklmnopqrstu
vwxyz

1 2 3 4 5 6 7 8 9 0

A HIGH RESOLUTION FILE OF THIS SPECIMEN SHEET CAN BE DOWNLOADED FROM THE VAULT EDITIONS' WEBSITE.

Vault Editions Ltd

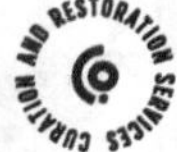

PRACTICE MAKES PERFECT

INDUSTRY STD

VAULTEDITIONS.COM

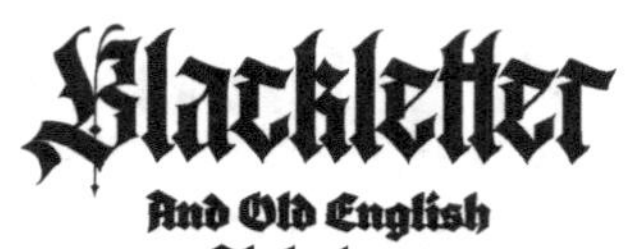
Blackletter
And Old English
Alphabets

ABCDEFGHIJRLMN
OPQRGTUVWXYZ
abcdefghijklmnopqrstuvwn
£&3
1234567890

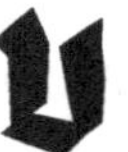
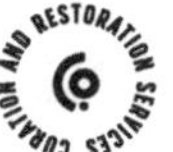
CURATION AND RESTORATION SERVICES

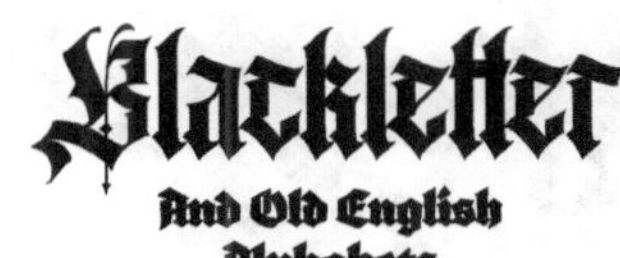

.TYPEFACE.
CAT ZENTENAER
FRAKTUR

| UPPER \| LOWER \| NUMERALS | ⟷ | WEIGHT: REGULAR | ⟷ | POINT SIZE: 82 |

A HIGH RESOLUTION FILE OF THIS SPECIMEN SHEET CAN BE DOWNLOADED FROM THE VAULT EDITIONS' WEBSITE.

Vault Editions Ltd

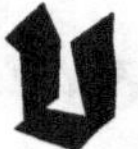

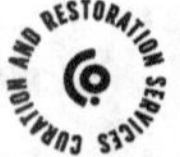

PRACTICE
MAKES
PERFECT
T R D · MRK

INDUSTRY STD

VAULTEDITIONS.COM

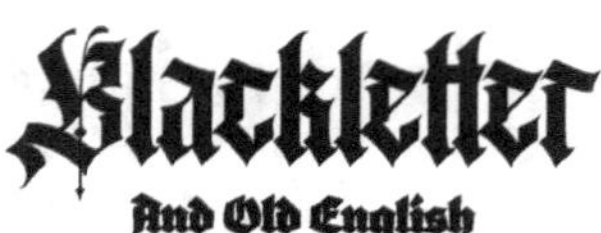

Blackletter
And Old English
Alphabets

105

ABCDEFGGGEEJKLMN
OPQRSTUVWXYZ

abcdefghijklmnopq
rstuvwxyz

1234567890

Vault Editions Ltd

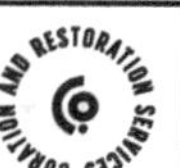

PRACTICE
MAKES
PERFECT
TRD   MRK

INDUSTRY STD

VAULTEDITIONS.COM

UPPER | LOWER | NUMERALS   WEIGHT: REGULAR   POINT SIZE: 81

ABCDEFGHIJKLM
NOPQRSTUVWXYZ

abcdefghijklmnopqrstuvwxyz

1234567890

A HIGH RESOLUTION FILE OF THIS SPECIMEN SHEET CAN BE DOWNLOADED FROM THE VAULT EDITIONS' WEBSITE.

Vault Editions Ltd

PRACTICE MAKES PERFECT

INDUSTRY STD

VAULTEDITIONS.COM

.DESIGNER.

PETER WIEGEL

Blackletter
And Old English
Alphabets

.TYPEFACE.

BARLOESIUS SCHRIFT

UPPER | LOWER | NUMERALS ⟷ WEIGHT: REGULAR ⟷ POINT SIZE: 82

ABCDEFGHIJKLM
NOPQRSTUVWXYZ
abcdefghijklmnopqrstu
vwxyz
1234567890

Vault Editions Ltd

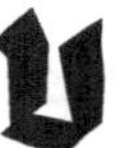

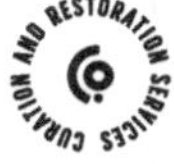

PRACTICE
MAKES
PERFECT
TRD MRK

INDUSTRY STD

VAULTEDITIONS.COM

108

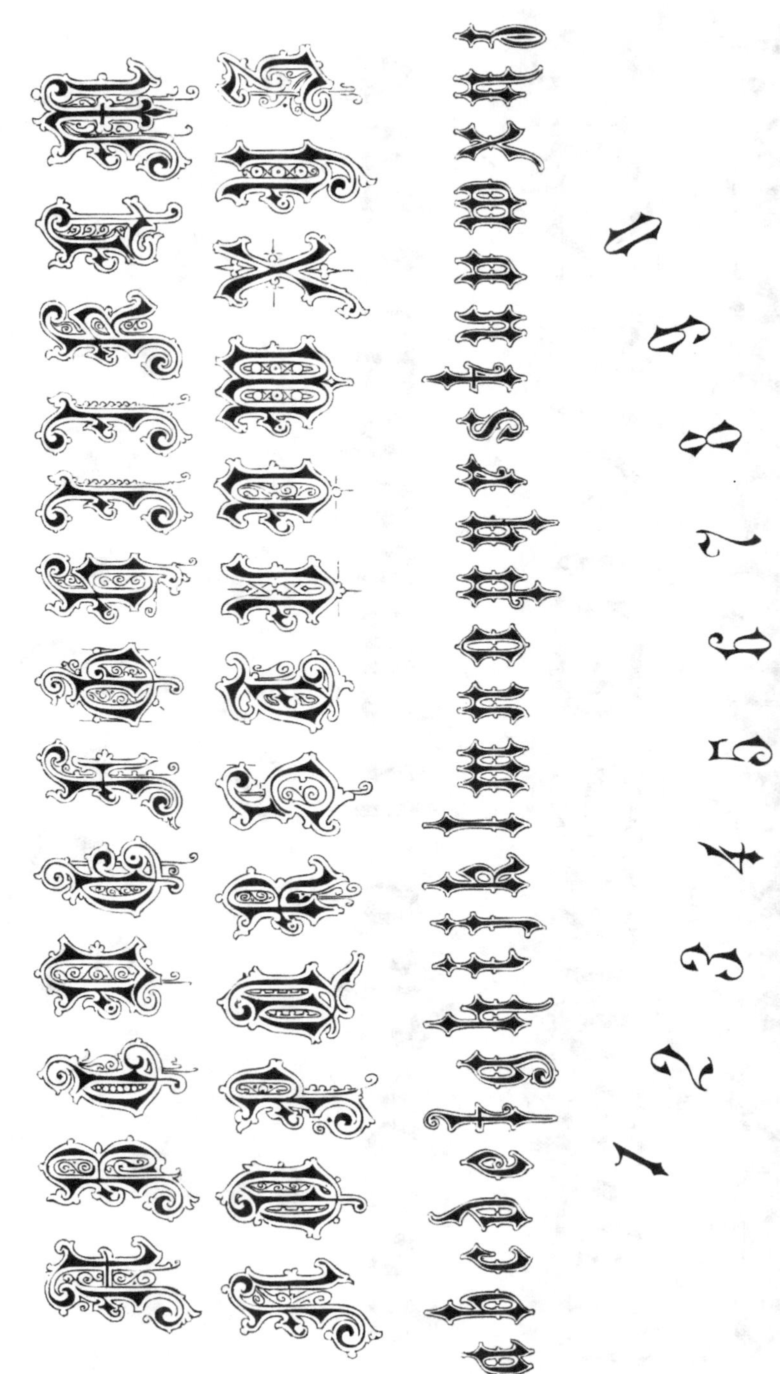

A HIGH RESOLUTION FILE OF THIS SPECIMEN SHEET CAN BE DOWNLOADED FROM THE VAULT EDITIONS' WEBSITE.

Vault Editions Ltd

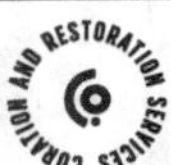

CURATION AND RESTORATION SERVICES

PRACTICE MAKES PERFECT
TRD · MRK

INDUSTRY STD

VAULTEDITIONS.COM

·DESIGNER·
PETER WIEGEL

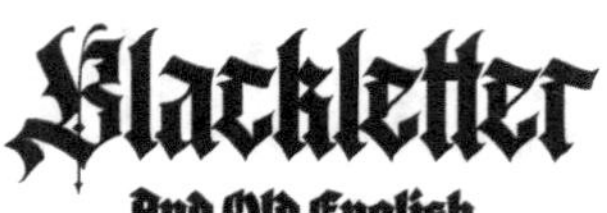

Blackletter
And Old English
Alphabets

·TYPEFACE·
SCHWABEN ALT

UPPER | LOWER | NUMERALS   ⟷   WEIGHT: BOLD   ⟷   POINT SIZE: 82

ABCDEFGHJJKLM
NOPQRSTUVWXYZ
abcdefghijklmnopqrsftuv
wxyz
1234567890

Vault Editions Ltd

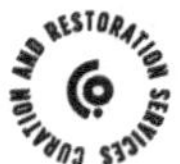

CURATION AND RESTORATION SERVICES · C ·

PRACTICE MAKES PERFECT
T R D   M R K

INDUSTRY STD

VAULTEDITIONS.COM

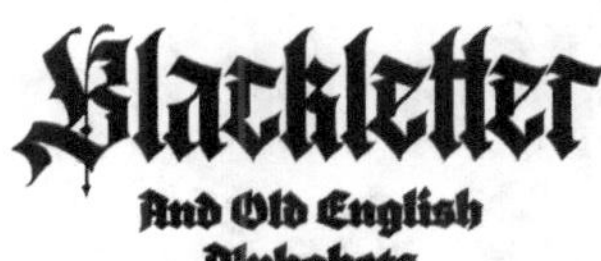

.DESIGNER.
PETER WIEGEL

.TYPEFACE.
ROTUNDA POMMERANIA

UPPER | LOWER | NUMERALS   ← →   WEIGHT: REGULAR   ← →   POINT SIZE: 81

ABCDEFGHIJKLM
NOPQRSTUVWXYZ
abcdefghijklmnopqrstuvw
xyz
1234567890

Vault Editions Ltd

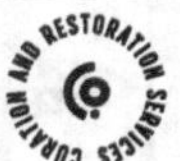

PRACTICE MAKES PERFECT
TRD MRK

INDUSTRY STD

VAULTEDITIONS.COM

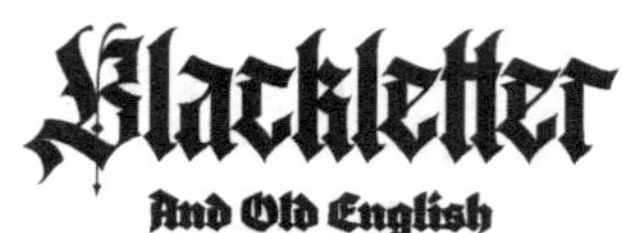

UPPER | LOWER | NUMERALS   ←→   WEIGHT: REGULAR   ←→   POINT SIZE: 82

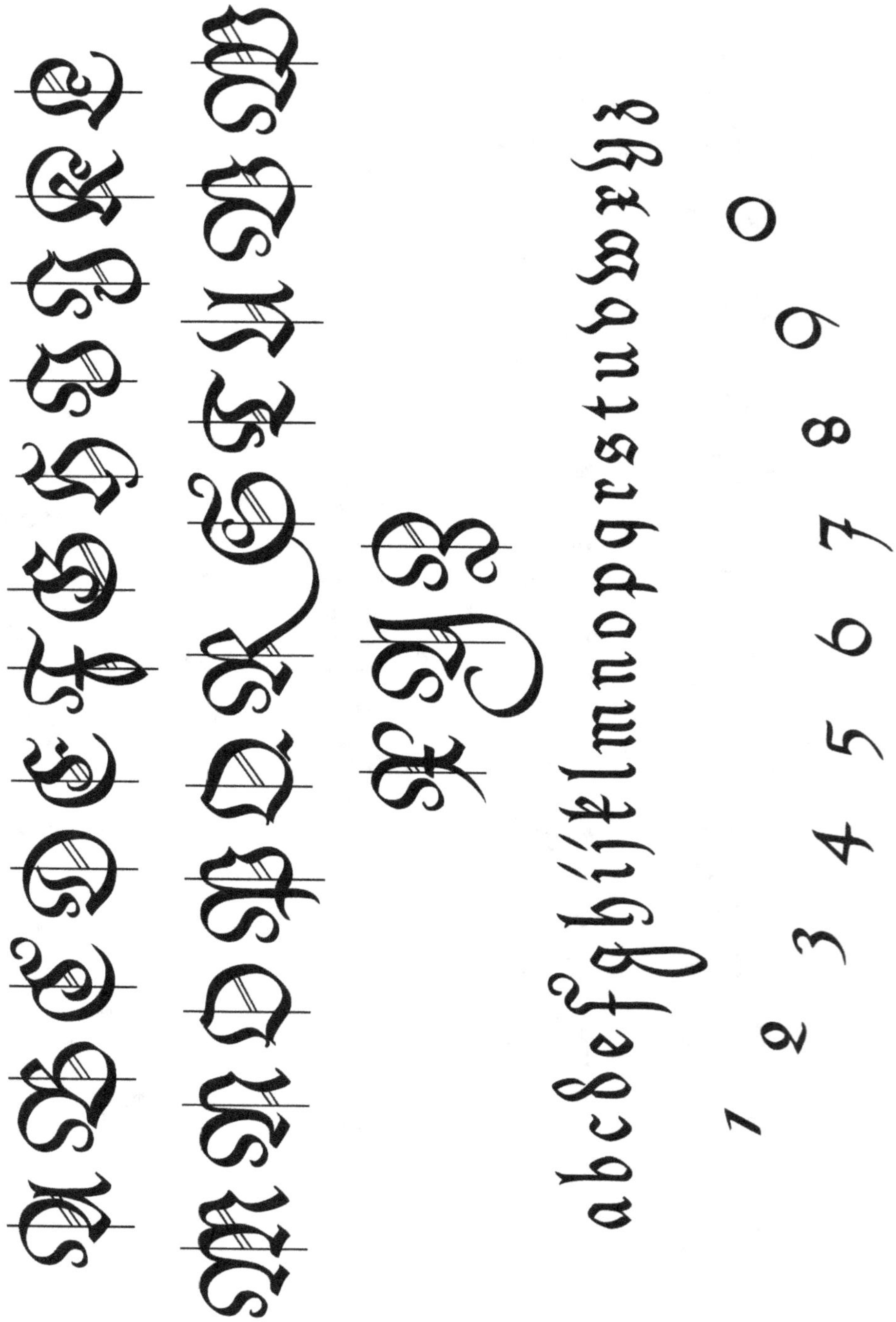

111

A HIGH RESOLUTION FILE OF THIS SPECIMEN SHEET CAN BE DOWNLOADED FROM THE VAULT EDITIONS' WEBSITE.

Vault Editions Ltd

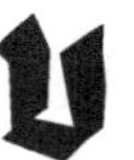

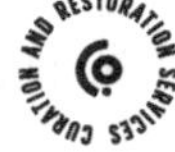

PRACTICE MAKES PERFECT

INDUSTRY STD

VAULTEDITIONS.COM

UPPER | LOWER | NUMERALS ⟷ **WEIGHT: REGULAR** ⟷ **POINT SIZE: 82**

ABCDEFGHIJKLM
NOPQRSTUVWXYZ
abcdefghijklmnopqrstuv
wxyz

1234567890

Vault Editions Ltd  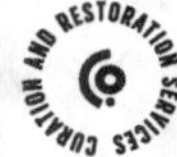

PRACTICE MAKES PERFECT

INDUSTRY STD

VAULTEDITIONS.COM

UPPER | LOWER | NUMERALS ← → WEIGHT: REGULAR ← → POINT SIZE: 83

113

A B C D E F G H I J K
L M N O P Q R S T
U V W X Y Z

a b c d e f g h i j k l m n o p q r s t u v w x y z

1 2 3 4 5 6 7 8 9 0

Vault Editions Ltd

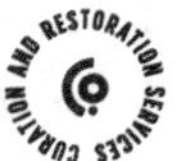

CURATION AND RESTORATION SERVICES

PRACTICE MAKES PERFECT
TRD · MRK

INDUSTRY STD

VAULTEDITIONS.COM

.DESIGNER.
PETER WIEGEL

Blackletter
And Old English Alphabets

.TYPEFACE.
POMMERN GOTISCH

UPPER | LOWER | NUMERALS — WEIGHT: REGULAR — POINT SIZE: 83

Vault Editions Ltd

CURATION AND RESTORATION SERVICES

PRACTICE MAKES PERFECT TRD MRK

INDUSTRY STD

VAULTEDITIONS.COM

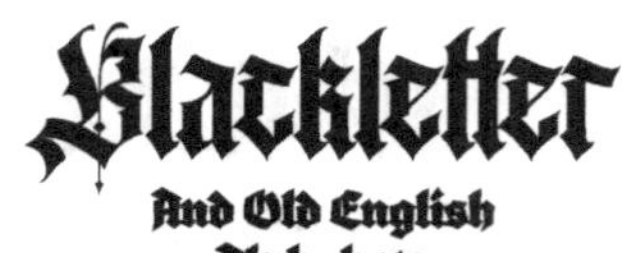

.TYPEFACE.
MODERNE FETTE
SCHWABACHER

UPPER | LOWER | NUMERALS ⟷ WEIGHT: REGULAR ⟷ POINT SIZE: 82

115

ABCDEFGHIJKLM
NOPQRSTUVWXYZ
abcdefghijklmnopqrsftuv
wxyz
1 2 3 4 5 6 7 8 9 0

Vault Editions Ltd

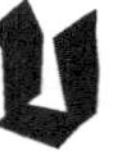
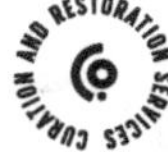

INDUSTRY STD
VAULTEDITIONS.COM

.DESIGNER.
PETER WIEGEL

Blackletter
And Old English
Alphabets

.TYPEFACE.
MODERNE SCHWABACHER
SHADOW

UPPER | LOWER | NUMERALS   ⟷   WEIGHT: REGULAR   ⟷   POINT SIZE: 82

A HIGH RESOLUTION FILE OF THIS SPECIMEN SHEET CAN BE DOWNLOADED FROM THE VAULT EDITIONS' WEBSITE.

Vault Editions Ltd

CURATION AND RESTORATION SERVICES

PRACTICE MAKES PERFECT
TRD   MRK

INDUSTRY STD

VAULTEDITIONS.COM

117

A HIGH RESOLUTION FILE OF THIS SPECIMEN SHEET CAN BE DOWNLOADED FROM THE VAULT EDITIONS' WEBSITE.

Vault Editions Ltd

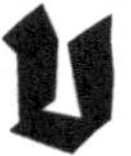
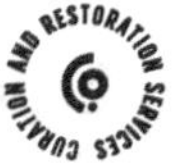

PRACTICE MAKES PERFECT

INDUSTRY STD

VAULTEDITIONS.COM

.DESIGNER.
PETER WIEGEL

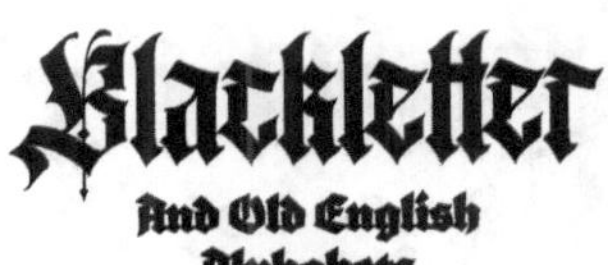

Blackletter
And Old English
Alphabets

.TYPEFACE.
MANUSKRIPT GOTHISCH

UPPER | LOWER | NUMERALS ⟷ WEIGHT: REGULAR ⟷ POINT SIZE: 81

Vault Editions Ltd

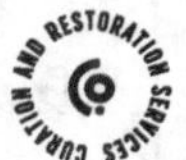

PRACTICE MAKES PERFECT

INDUSTRY STD

VAULTEDITIONS.COM

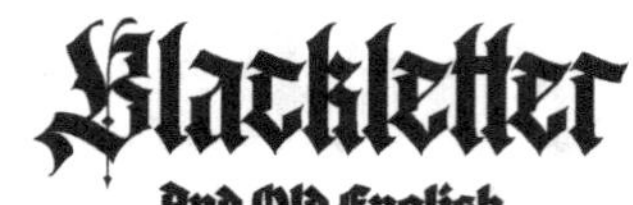
Blackletter
And Old English
Alphabets

UPPER | LOWER | NUMERALS | WEIGHT: REGULAR | POINT SIZE: 82

119

ABCDEFGHIJKLM
NOPQRSTUVWXYZ
abcdefghijklmno
pqrstuvwxyz
1234567890

A HIGH RESOLUTION FILE OF THIS SPECIMEN SHEET CAN BE DOWNLOADED FROM THE VAULT EDITIONS' WEBSITE.

Vault Editions Ltd

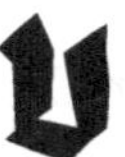

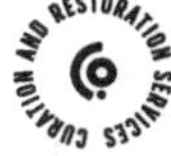

CURATION AND RESTORATION SERVICES

PRACTICE MAKES PERFECT
TRD · MRK

INDUSTRY STD

VAULTEDITIONS.COM

.DESIGNER.
JOSEPH WARREN PHINNEY

Blackletter
And Old English Alphabets

.TYPEFACE.
BRADLEY GRATIS

UPPER | LOWER | NUMERALS ⟷ WEIGHT: REGULAR ⟷ POINT SIZE: 83

ABCDEFGHIJKLMN
OPQRSCUVWXYZ

abcdefghijklmnopqrst
uvwxyz

1234567890

Vault Editions Ltd

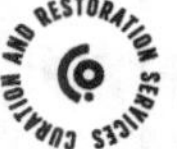

PRACTICE MAKES PERFECT

INDUSTRY STD

VAULTEDITIONS.COM

121

Vault Editions Ltd

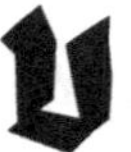

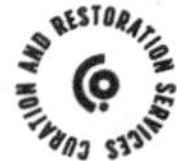

INDUSTRY STD

VAULTEDITIONS.COM

·DESIGNER·

KEVIN KING

Blackletter
And Old English
Alphabets

·TYPEFACE·

KINGTHINGS SPIKE

UPPER | LOWER | NUMERALS ⟷ WEIGHT: REGULAR ⟷ POINT SIZE: 83

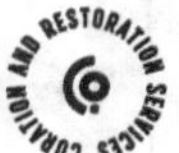

A HIGH RESOLUTION FILE OF THIS SPECIMEN SHEET CAN BE DOWNLOADED FROM THE VAULT EDITIONS' WEBSITE.

Vault Editions Ltd

CURATION AND RESTORATION SERVICES

PRACTICE MAKES PERFECT

INDUSTRY STD

VAULTEDITIONS.COM

·DESIGNER·
J. MACH WUST

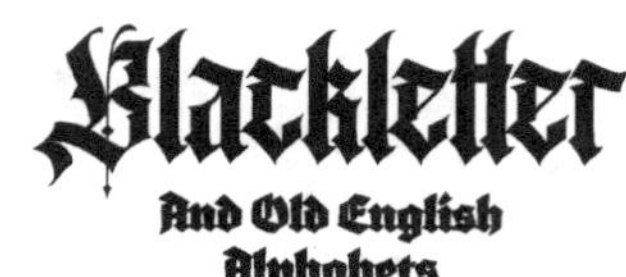

Blackletter
And Old English
Alphabets

·TYPEFACE·
UNI FRAKTUR COOK

UPPER | LOWER | NUMERALS ⟷ WEIGHT: REGULAR ⟷ POINT SIZE: 82

Vault Editions Ltd

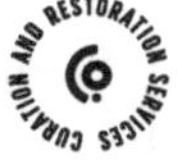

PRACTICE
MAKES
PERFECT
T·R·D   M·R·K

INDUSTRY STD

VAULTEDITIONS.COM

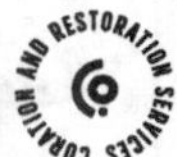

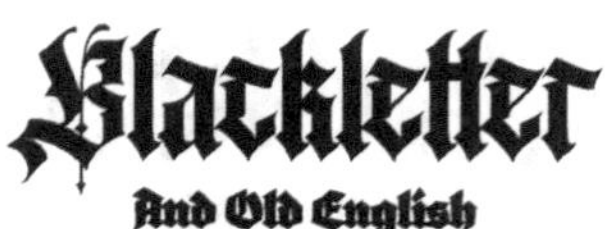

UPPER | LOWER | NUMERALS — WEIGHT: REGULAR — POINT SIZE: 82

125

Vault Editions Ltd

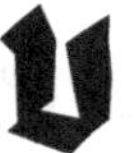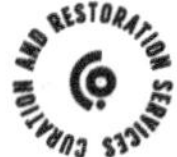

CURATION AND RESTORATION SERVICES

PRACTICE
MAKES
PERFECT
TRD MRK

INDUSTRY STD
VAULTEDITIONS.COM

.DESIGNER.
FREDRICH R. BRENNAN

Blackletter
And Old English
Alphabets

.TYPEFACE.
CHOMSKY

UPPER | LOWER | NUMERALS   WEIGHT: REGULAR   POINT SIZE: 82

ABCDEFGHIJKL
MNOPQRSTUVW
XYZ

abcdefghijklmnopqrstu
vwxyz

1234567890

Vault Editions Ltd

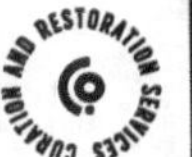

CURATION AND RESTORATION SERVICES

PRACTICE MAKES PERFECT

INDUSTRY STD

VAULTEDITIONS.COM

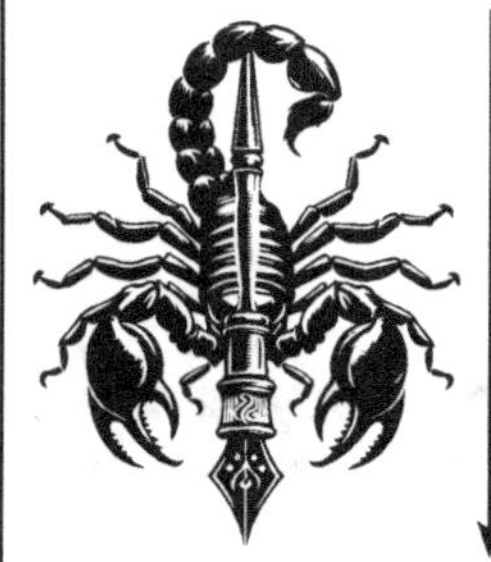

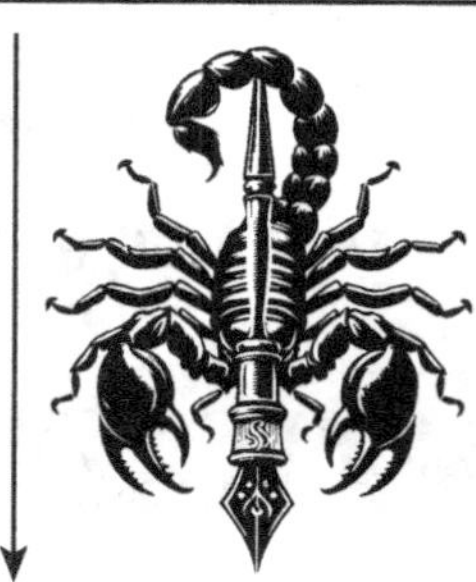

01
VOLUME

V A U L T   E D I T I O N S

VAULT EDITIONS

This publication is a new work created by Vault Editions Ltd

DOWNLOAD YOUR FILES

Follow the instructions below to access your downloadable files

LEARN MORE

At Vault Editions, our mission is to create the world's most comprehensive collection of image archives for the practical use of artists and designers. If you have enjoyed this book, you can discover more of our titles at vaulteditions.com

REVIEW THIS BOOK

As a family-owned and operated independent publisher, reviews are essential to the success of our business. Please leave an honest review of this book wherever you purchased it.

JOIN OUR COMMUNITY

Are you the creative and curious type? If so, you will love our community on Instagram. Every day, we share bizarre and beautiful artwork ranging from 17th and 18th-century natural history and scientific illustrations to mythical beasts, ornamental designs, anatomical drawings and more; join our community of 280K+ people today by searching @vault_editions on Instagram.

STEP ONE

Enter the following web address on a desktop or laptop computer in your web browser.

vaulteditions.com/pages/bla

STEP TWO

Enter the following password to access the download page:

bla234747838sxda

STEP THREE

Follow the prompts to access your high-resolution files.

CONTACT

For all technical enquiries, please contact: info@vaulteditions.com

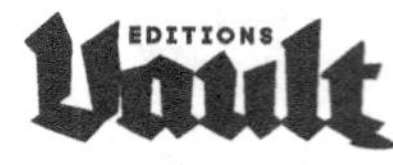